TABLE OF CONTENTS

BOXES

TABLES

FIGURES

FOREWORD

THE MISSION OF THE MULTILATERAL INVESTMENT GUARANTEE AGENCY (MIGA) IS TO PROMOTE FOREIGN DIRECT INVESTMENT (FDI) INTO DEVELOPING COUNTRIES TO SUPPORT ECONOMIC GROWTH, REDUCE POVERTY, AND IMPROVE PEOPLE'S LIVES. AS PART OF THIS MANDATE, THE AGENCY SEEKS TO FOSTER A BETTER UNDERSTANDING OF INVESTOR PERCEPTIONS OF POLITICAL RISK AS THEY RELATE TO FDI, AS WELL AS THE ROLE OF THE POLITICAL RISK INSURANCE (PRI) INDUSTRY IN MITIGATING THESE RISKS.

The global economic and financial crisis has severely curtailed economic growth and international private capital flows, prompting unprecedented government interventions. Although developing countries have not been spared, past economic and policy reforms, growing domestic markets and emergency financial assistance have helped them weather the storm.

In the current context of high uncertainty and relative retreat of the private sector, this report seeks to examine the evolution of political risk perceptions. Understanding how investors perceive and deal with these perils will contribute to mapping out the role of political risk insurance in the emerging post-crisis investment landscape, and how it can contribute to a revival of FDI. With scarcer private capital and only a handful of countries absorbing the majority of investment flows to emerging markets, encouraging private capital to the world's poorest economies remains a critical focus for the World Bank Group.

The report focuses on how the current global financial crisis has impacted the outlook of the investment community and the insurance industry regarding investments in developing countries. For this purpose, MIGA commissioned independent agencies to conduct several corporate surveys. More specifically, the report examines: (i) overall trends in FDI and political risk perceptions; (ii) corporate views on foreign investment and the political risk environment in emerging markets; and (iii) the ability of the PRI industry to respond to an emerging post-crisis investment landscape. Given the changing shape of the world economy and MIGA's mandate, the report pays particular attention to the growing role of South-based investors and PRI providers in promoting global cross-border investment flows.

Izumi Kobayashi
Executive Vice President

ACKNOWLEDGEMENTS

This report was prepared by a team led by Stephan Dreyhaupt, and including Emanuel Salinas, Persephone Economou, Moina Varkie-Toft and Thomas Tichar. Inputs were also received from Roxanna Faily, Alpona Banerji, and Caroline Lambert, who also edited the report. Suzanne Pelland was in charge of graphic design. Melissa Johnson provided administrative support.

This report would not have been possible without the vision and support of James Bond, MIGA's Chief Operating Officer. The team also wishes to thank the other members of the editorial committee, including Frank Lysy, Edith Quintrell, Marcus Williams, Daniel Villar, Marc Roex, Mallory Saleson, Mansoor Dailami, and Jonathan Halpern, for providing invaluable guidance and comments. Throughout the various stages of the report, the team was fortunate to have the cooperation of the World Bank's Development Prospects Group (DECPG) under the guidance of Mansoor Dailami. We would also like to thank MIGA colleagues, in particular Srilal Perera and Ivan Illescas.

The World Bank's Development Economics Vice Presidency (DEC) provided most of the macroeconomic data used in chapter 1, as well as comments on the analysis. UNCTAD contributed information on trends in international investment agreements. The investor surveys covered in chapters 1 and 2 were conducted on behalf of MIGA by the Economist Intelligence Unit (global survey) and the Vale Columbia Center on Sustainable International Investment (BRIC survey). Additional perspectives of Singapore-based investors were obtained with the help of International Enterprise (IE) Singapore. The BRIC survey also relied on contributions from Sociedade Brasileira de Estudos de Empresas Transnacionais e da Globalização Econômica (SOBEET) in Brazil; Qi Guoqiang, President, International Cooperation Journal, Ministry of Commerce, in China; Premila Nazareth, an independent consultant in India; and Andrei Panibratov at the Graduate School of Management, St. Petersburg State University in Russia. Chapter 3 benefited from invaluable co-operation from Kimberly Wiehl and Lennart Skarp of the Berne Union. In addition, inputs were received from the African Trade Insurance Agency, Charles Berry of BPL Global and Toby Heppel of FirstCity Partnership Ltd.

Peer reviews were provided by Carlos Alberto Primo Braga (Director, Economic Policy and Debt in the Poverty Reduction and Economic Management Network, World Bank), Pierre Guislain (Director, Investment Climate Department, World Bank), Henry Russell (Manager, Finance and Guarantees Group, World Bank), Hans Timmer (Director, Development Prospects Group, World Bank), Karl P. Sauvant (Executive Director, Vale Columbia Center on Sustainable International Investment), James Zhan (Director, Division on Investment and Enterprise, UNCTAD) and Michael Gestrin (Senior Economist and GFI Programme Manager, Investment Division, OECD). Additional comments were received from David Neckar (Willis), Kevin Godier (Global Trade Review), Joerg Weber (Chief, Programme International Arrangements Section, UNCTAD), Jan Muller, Thomas Meyer (Hannover Re), Daniel Hui (Swiss Re), Christina Deischl and Petra Hansen (Munich Re).

SELECTED ABBREVIATIONS

ATI	African Trade Insurance Agency
BIT	Bilateral investment treaty
BRIC	Brazil, the Russian Federation, India and China
BU	Berne Union
CDS	Credit default swaps
CIS	Commonwealth of Independent States
ECA	Export credit agency
ECGC	Export Credit Guarantee Corporation
EIU	Economist Intelligence Unit
FDI	Foreign direct investment
GDP	Gross domestic product
ICIEC	Islamic Corporation for the Insurance of Investment and Export Credit
ICSID	International Centre for Settlement of Investment Disputes
IMF	International Monetary Fund
M&As	Mergers and acquisitions
MIGA	Multilateral Investment Guarantee Agency
MNE	Multinational enterprise
OECD	Organisation for Economic Co-operation and Development
OPIC	Overseas Private Investment Corporation
PRI	Political risk insurance
T&C	Currency transfer and convertibility
VCC	Vale Columbia Center on Sustainable International Investment

EXECUTIVE SUMMARY

Political risk is a top concern for corporate foreign investors—from industrialized but also developing countries—when venturing into emerging markets. At the same time, these investors maintain a positive outlook on economic and business prospects in the developing world, which is expected to attract a growing share of global foreign direct investment (FDI) as the world economy slowly recovers. Positive business sentiment over emerging markets amid concerns over political perils point to a sustained need to mitigate these perils. This, added to the rise of South-based investors, offers opportunities and challenges for the political risk insurance (PRI) industry. In the current context of high uncertainty, understanding how investors perceive and deal with political risks helps to map out the role of PRI in the emerging post-crisis investment landscape.

This report focuses on FDI and PRI for long-term investment, and only covers political risk in developing

MAJOR CONSTRAINTS ON FOREIGN INVESTMENT IN EMERGING MARKETS
Percent of respondents

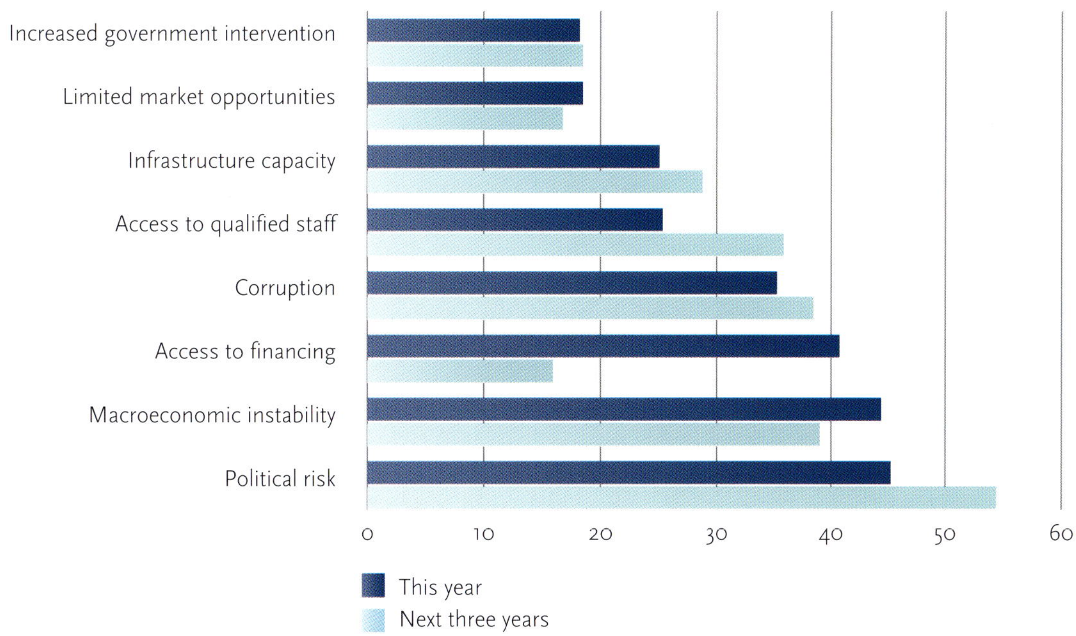

In your opinion, which of the following factors will pose the greatest constraint on investments by your company in emerging markets this year and over the next three years?

Source: MIGA-EIU Political Risk Survey 2009.
Note: Percentages add up to more than 100 percent due to multiple selections.

countries. Although political risk also affects other forms of private capital flows, these are beyond the scope of this publication.

The main findings of the report are summarized as follows:

While political risks top foreign investors' concerns, the global economic and financial crisis has not fundamentally altered FDI prospects for emerging markets.

Political risk remains one of the main obstacles to foreign investment in emerging markets and is likely to continue being so over the medium term. Corporate investors surveyed for this report rank political risk amongst their top three concerns when investing in developing countries more often than any other consideration, including macroeconomic stability and access to financing. The survey suggests that the prominence of political risk relative to other concerns will increase over the next three years, as constraints related to the global financial and economic crisis gradually ease.

Booming economies, abundant liquidity, shrinking financial spreads, flattening risk premiums and a hunt for higher returns encouraged a relatively high tolerance for risk over the past few years. Yet some political risks were already deteriorating before the economic crisis hit. Contract renegotiations in extractive industries and a resurgence of "resource nationalism" in some places heightened concerns over expropriation and breach of contract, even though the nature of expropriation risk has evolved from the outright nationalizations prevalent in the 1970s to regulatory takings. Decentralization has introduced sub-sovereign entities as a source of risk, in particular for infrastructure projects whose viability relies on these entities being able to meet their contractual and financial obligations. Controls on access to foreign exchange have receded and financial markets have been liberalized over the past two decades, but some concerns over the ability to convert and transfer currency in times of crisis, such as the current one, persist, particularly in fixed exchange regimes. High-profile terrorist attacks around the world, as well as piracy and separatist, ethnic or religious tensions in some countries, have highlighted that the risk of political violence is still prevalent. At the same time, the shift of global FDI towards emerging markets, perceived to be riskier than industrialized ones, may have contributed to the salience of political risks, with investors expanding their investment horizons to unfamiliar business destinations.

These trends are likely to persist over the medium term. As the world economy recovers, some form of resource nationalism may endure in certain countries. Opportunities for private investment in infrastructure and the extractive industries, with their long term horizons, large scale, and reliance on central or local government licenses or guarantees will continue to carry concerns over breach of contract, expropriation and related political risks. Some forms of political violence, such as terrorism and civil unrest, are not expected to ease in the short or medium term. And the continued globalization of capital flows still carries the potential to destabilize exchange rates regimes and local financial markets, providing temptations for some governments to restrict these flows in times of crisis.

The recent economic and financial turbulence does not appear to have altered political risk perceptions across the board, but rather exacerbated concerns over specific perils and destinations for a minority of investors. A majority of the investors surveyed for this report do not believe the downturn itself resulted in higher political risks in their main investment destinations; 35 percent, however, thought otherwise. Specific political risks directly related to the fallout of the crisis have emerged in the most vulnerable destinations. Concerns that governments may be tempted to impose transfer and convertibility restrictions have emerged in countries where the financial

Investors' views on foreign investment plans
Percent of respondents

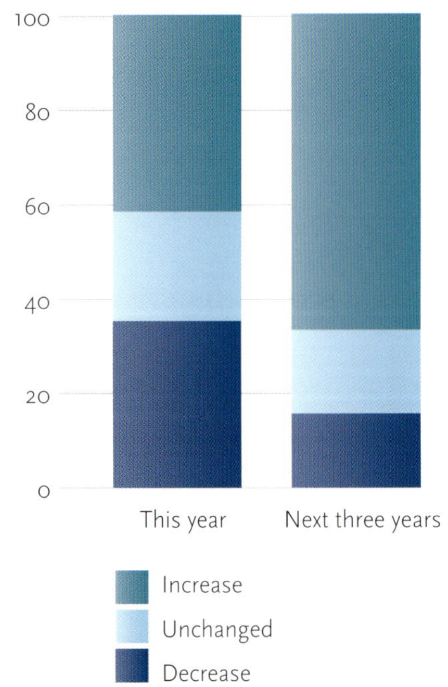

Do you expect your planned investments abroad to change this year compared with last year, and over the next three years compared with the previous three years?

Source: MIGA-EIU Political Risk Survey 2009.

crisis has severely undermined liquidity and put pressure on the local currency. With unemployment on the rise, declining remittances and pressure on social programs due to shrinking government revenues, the risk of civil unrest is more pronounced in some countries. Budgetary pressures have also raised concerns about the ability of governments and state-owned entities to fulfill their contractual obligations and honor sovereign guarantees. Better policy regulatory environments, stimulus packages, and international assistance, however, have somewhat cushioned the impact of the downturn, and these risks have so far either not materialized, or have had a limited impact. In addition, they are expected ease as the economy slowly recovers.

Although the global financial crisis and economic downturn have severely curtailed economic growth and FDI, global foreign investment flows are expected to start recovering in 2010. Longer-term trends that sustained the rise of FDI to record levels until 2008—including the corporate search of new markets, resources and assets, intensified competition, the development of global supply chains, liberalized investment regimes and lucrative investment opportunities—are expected to sustain foreign investment once the global economy recovers from the recent shock. The investor survey conducted for this report confirms that, despite the severity of the global crisis, foreign investment intentions are robust over the medium term; if signs of economic recovery were to stall or reverse, however, or constraints on project finance to persist, these FDI intentions may struggle to materialize in full.

The developing world remains an attractive destination for FDI. Although emerging markets have not been spared from the effects of the crisis, they have on average fared better than the industrialized world in terms of both economic growth and FDI inflows. Whereas the economies of industrialized countries are projected to contract by 3.2 percent in 2009, developing countries' GDP is expected to still grow by 1.2 percent. Emerging markets are expected to keep capturing and generating an increasing share of global FDI going forward, a trend that predates the crisis. The surveys conducted for this report confirm that investors' outlook on emerging markets remains bullish; investment intentions that emerge from these surveys, however, remain heavily focused on the handful of countries—particularly Brazil, the Russian Federation, India and China (BRICs)—that have absorbed the bulk of FDI into developing economies over the past few years. Added to the continued rise of investors based in emerging markets, this underscores an economic shift towards the emerging world, whose weight in the global economy is expected to continue growing.

Interest in PRI

Percent of respondents

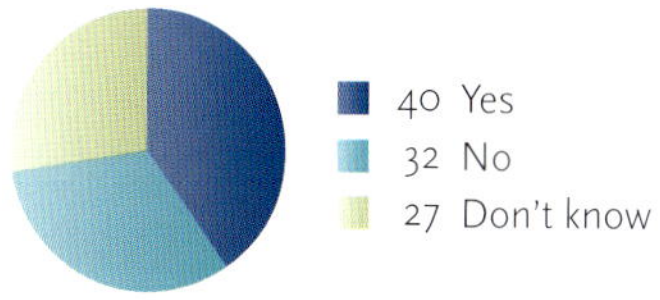

Moving forward, do you expect your company to consider political risk insurance for its investments abroad?

Source: MIGA-EIU Political Risk Survey 2009.

Concerns over political risks, combined with sustained FDI into emerging markets over the medium term, suggest a growing need for political risk mitigation and opportunities for the PRI industry.

The continued prominence of political risk concerns and the growing interest in emerging markets as investment destinations underpin interest in risk mitigation going forward. Historically, political risk insurance has covered only a small share of FDI, as most investments into emerging markets have been uninsured. Yet only 6 percent of investors surveyed for this report said they did not mitigate political risks at all; but those who did manage these risks appear to rely primarily on their own risk management capacity—even though a sizable minority judges that capacity as poor—and on informal mitigation mechanisms, such as engaging with local governments or local partners. Insurance, on the other hand, appears to be a niche product: 14 percent of surveyed investors contracted PRI, but almost twice as many did so when venturing into markets considered the riskiest. However, 40 percent of the respondents also indicated they would consider using insurance for future investments.

This places the PRI industry in a position to expand its reach and support the expected rebound of FDI to the developing world. The industry has grown from a minimal presence 20 years ago to a well-established market today, generating annual premiums of about $1 billion. The sector is now mature and resilient, shaped by numerous shocks, such as the Argentine peso crisis and the September 11 attacks, in the past two decades. Its exposure is diversified across a number of well-capitalized and informed carriers, underwriting standards and processes have been strengthened, and reinsurance has grown exponentially.

So far, the PRI industry has weathered the global downturn relatively well: most private and public members of the Berne Union have reported robust financial results, in spite of a decline in new business in the first half of 2009; the downturn has so far not resulted in the expected level of claims; and overall market capacity for political risk cover appears to have held steady.

The financial crisis has resulted in higher selectivity and stricter underwriting conditions in some segments of the private insurance market though, and capacity has been reduced for some countries. The multilateral and national insurers, however, are better able to maintain capacity, prices and tenors in times of crisis, and are therefore well placed to fill potential gaps that may arise in the private market. This highlights public insurers' role in stabilizing the PRI market in uncertain times. Continued cooperation between public and private insurers—through coinsurance, reinsurance and information sharing—will be important to support the expected recovery in FDI. The industry as a whole is well able to respond to an increase in demand for risk mitigation that may arise from investors deciding to insure existing projects, as well as from the revival in new investments expected from 2010 onwards.

Although prospects for FDI are optimistic, banks are likely to remain cautious, at least in the near term, potentially constraining investments relying on project finance. This could affect demand for PRI in conflicting ways when it comes to these types of projects: a lower volume of operations on the one hand, but a higher willingness to obtain PRI for projects that do go ahead.

The emergence of South-based investors is increasingly shaping the global FDI environment and presents regional growth opportunities, but also challenges, for the PRI industry.

South-based investors, particularly from the BRICs, have been a growing source of investment to emerging markets, and this trend is expected to continue over the medium term. Between 2003 and 2008, FDI outflows from developing countries increased more than eight fold, reaching an estimated $198 billion in 2008, 73 percent of which came from BRIC countries. With their economies having so far weathered the crisis better than industrialized ones, the South-based investors surveyed for this report appeared bullish in their investment plans.

These emerging investors are also concerned about political risks: the surveys conducted for this report show

Net FDI outflows from developing countries 2000-2008

$ billion

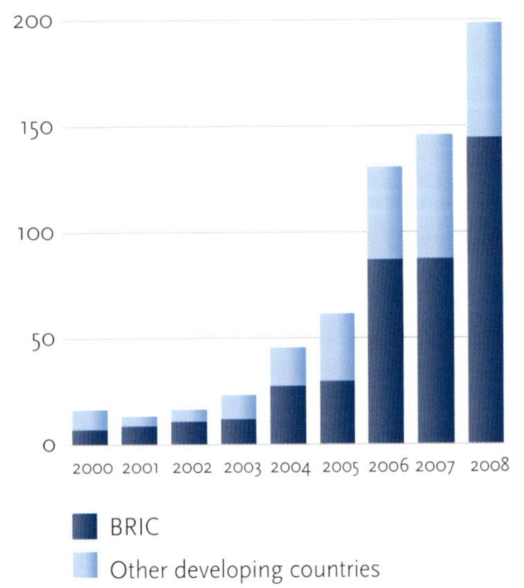

Source: World Bank 2009, and latest revised estimates.

Share of South-based investment insurance providers in new business*

$ billion

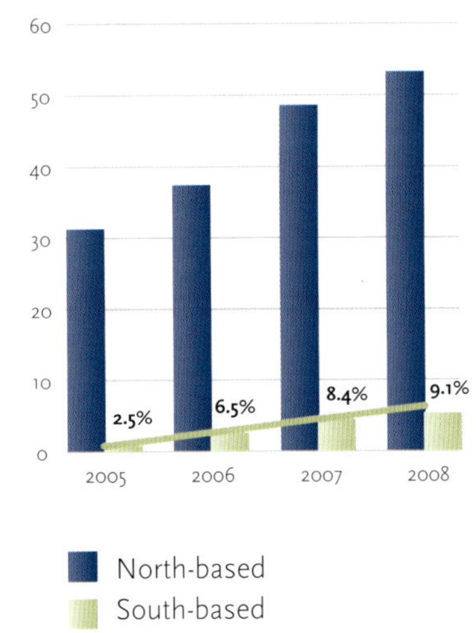

* *Berne Union members only.*

Source: Berne Union 2009.

that, as with North-based investors, political risk is ranked first amongst concerns when investing in emerging markets, both today and over the medium term. As they venture from familiar regions, South-based investors appear to be increasingly more preoccupied with political perils relative to other concerns.

Most South-based respondents use some form of risk mitigation but, when they do, favor informal methods such as engaging with local governments and setting up joint ventures, rather than PRI. Yet over half the survey respondents—in particular those from China and India—indicated they would consider political risk insurance for future investments.

The growing weight of South-based investors in global FDI offers opportunities and challenges for the PRI industry. Insurers are reaching out to this fast-growing market segment. The private PRI market has been developing a growing presence outside of London, New York and Bermuda to capture the rising demand for investment insurance from South-based investors; Singapore, for example, is emerging as a regional insurance hub. The changing landscape of global FDI is also shaping the industry, as some PRI providers originating from emerging markets are fast expanding their investment cover. South-based export-credit agencies such as Sinosure have increased their investment insurance portfolios manifold, and relatively new regional insurers such as the African Trade Insurance Agency (ATI) have also experienced tremendous growth in the past few years. New products specifically tailored to local needs—such as Shariah-compliant insurance, have been developed. The share of South-based insurers in Berne Union members' new business expanded from 2.5 percent in 2005 to over 9.1 percent in 2008. But the market still needs to improve investor awareness of PRI and become more proactive in promoting its services and adapting its offerings to the needs of South-based investors.

FDI recovery, the growing interest in emerging markets as investment destinations and concerns over political risks are expected to support a further expansion of the PRI industry. But while it will most likely continue growing in absolute terms, PRI is likely to remain a niche product providing cover for a small share of FDI and project finance debt to emerging markets, in part because insurable risks are a subset of the total spectrum of political risks which concern investors. History suggests that PRI is of particular interest in the immediate aftermath of financial and economic crises, and following high-profile claims, when certain political risks are exposed.

Although PRI is not a key determinant of FDI flows to developing countries, it can nonetheless play a key role in supporting the changing dynamics of global investment, in facilitating large and complex projects in sectors that have high development impact and are government priorities, and in promoting investments into underserved markets, such as poorer countries and conflict-afflicted environments.

CHAPTER ONE

WORLD INVESTMENT TRENDS: *OUTLOOK AND CORPORATE PERSPECTIVES*

Overview

Until the recent economic downturn, private capital flows, especially FDI,[1] had surged to record levels in both developed and emerging markets. The financial crisis dented investment plans everywhere, pressing the brakes on global growth. Although developing countries have not been spared from the effects of the crisis, they have on average fared better than the industrialized world in terms of both economic growth and FDI inflows. In addition, trends that sustained the expansion of FDI before the downturn, such as the growing consumer markets, internationalization of supply chains and intensified competition, as well as increasingly open investment regimes, capital markets and business environments, are expected to underpin a revival of foreign investment.

FDI flows—projected to rebound in 2010—are expected to further swing towards emerging markets over time. This trend, also sustained by the rise of investors based in emerging markets, reflects an economic shift towards the emerging world, whose global weight is expected to continue growing both as a destination, but also as a source, of FDI.

Despite the severity of the crisis, corporate investors[2] have maintained a positive outlook on business prospects in emerging markets, according to a set of surveys of multinational enterprises (MNEs) carried out for this report. Investment intentions, however, remain heavily concentrated in the handful of countries that have absorbed the bulk of FDI into emerging markets over the past few years.

The Global Economy on the Way to Recovery

Well into its deepest global financial crisis of the post-war era, the world economy is entering a phase of economic recovery and financial market stabilization. Following extraordinary policy responses, financial market conditions are signaling much improved investor confidence and the return of risk appetite for emerging market assets. Since March 2009, liquidity conditions in global interbank markets have eased considerably, credit risk premiums have narrowed, and equity markets have staged a tentative revival. The pace of credit rating deterioration has slowed nearly to a halt in the emerging market sovereign class. According to Standard & Poor's, no emerging market sovereign has defaulted in the past six months, and one sovereign emerged from default.[3]

Led by the strong rebound in industrial production in Asia, the global economy appears to be moving to positive growth territory in the second half of 2009, although the recovery is expected to be much subdued. Global GDP is forecast to increase by a modest 2.6 percent in 2010 and 3.2 percent by 2011 (table 1.1), as banking sector consolidation, negative wealth effects, and risk aversion continue to weigh on demand throughout the forecast period.[4] In developing countries, growth rates are expected to be higher, at 5.1 percent and 5.6 percent, respectively, in 2010 and 2011. Given the output losses already absorbed, and because GDP is expected to reach its potential growth rate only by 2011, the output gap (the difference between actual GDP and its potential) and unemployment are expected to remain high, and recession-like conditions will continue to prevail. In addition, risks that the recovery may stall or reverse, especially as stimulus measures begin to unwind, could translate into a more pessimistic ecomonic scenario.

The policy agenda for placing the global financial markets on a stable footing and fostering a durable economic recovery remains challenging. Over the past two years, the world has seen how a negative feedback loop between financial instability and the real economy can unfold in a dramatic slump in world industrial production, trade and output. The intensification of the financial crisis in the fall of 2008 dramatically brought home this scenario.[5]

The World Bank estimates that the global economy contracted by 2.2 percent in 2009 (table 1.1). Global industrial production shrank by 13 percent in 2009 (year to year latest), and fixed investment by 9.8 percent. Unemployment has soared, and consumer confidence plummeted to all-time lows at the height of the crisis, while international trade contracted. Commodity prices (including internationally traded food commodities) also suffered, slumping by 36 percent between their peak in mid-2008 and April 2009, but have rebounded since then. Oil prices were also down by more than 70 percent in December 2008 from their peak in mid-2008, but have also recovered since then. Only consumer savings increased, as households cut back or delayed large expenditures in the face of rising uncertainty and negative wealth effects from falling equity and housing prices.

Developing countries, on average, have fared better than the industrialized world (table 1.1). They have overall managed to avoid sliding into a recession, and the World Bank estimates developing economies to have grown by 1.2 percent in 2009. Even excluding China and India, the economic contraction of 2.2 percent is less severe than the recession experienced in high-income countries.

Developing countries have been hit unevenly, however. Europe and Central Asia— heavily dependent on trade and investments from the European Union— was the hardest hit by the abrupt reversal of capital flows and

Table 1.1 The Global Economic Outlook, 2007-2011

Percentage change from previous year

Real GDP growth [a]	2007	2008	2009[e]	2010[f]	2011[f]
World	3.8	1.7	-2.2	2.6	3.2
High income	2.6	0.5	-3.2	1.7	2.3
Developing countries	7.6	5.7	1.2	5.1	5.6
East Asia and Pacific	10.1	8.0	6.7	8.2	8.2
Europe and Central Asia	7.1	4.3	-6.1	1.9	3.0
Latin America and Caribbean	5.5	3.9	-2.5	3.0	3.6
Middle East and North Africa	5.3	5.8	3.0	3.4	4.1
South Asia	8.5	5.7	5.3	6.4	6.6
Sub-Saharan Africa	6.5	4.9	0.7	3.8	4.9
Memorandum items					
Developing countries					
Excluding transition countries	7.6	5.7	2.5	5.6	6.0
Excluding China and India	6.1	4.4	-2.2	3.0	3.9

Source: World Bank 2009, and latest revised estimates.

[a] *GDP in 2005 constant dollars; 2005 prices and market exchange rates.*

[e] *Estimate*

[f] *Forecast*

weaker demand for exports. Latin America and the Caribbean has also suffered from the withdrawal of foreign funds, tumbling equity markets and plummeting exchange rates, but has weathered the crisis armed with stronger fiscal, currency and financial fundamentals than in the past. Other developing regions have managed to avoid recession altogether, even though their economic growth has slowed. With little direct exposure to the sources of financial crisis, but still affected through its integration with industrialized countries via trade and capital flows, the East Asia and Pacific region fared relatively well, as did South Asia. Although less directly affected by the crisis, growth in the Middle East and North Africa region slowed as local equity and property markets came under intense pressures, while Sub-Saharan Africa suffered from the decline in commodity prices.

As the global economy begins to recover in 2010, growth in developing economies is again forecast to outpace high-income countries'. East Asia and Pacific is expected to grow the fastest, followed by South Asia, and Sub-Saharan Africa. The biggest turnaround is expected to take place in those developing regions whose economies have suffered the most, namely, Europe and Central Asia, as well as Latin America and the Caribbean.

Trends in Foreign Direct Investment

The global financial and economic crisis has severely dented the surge of private capital flows to developing countries—including FDI—observed over the past decade (annex 1). Given its long-term nature, FDI has been more resilient than other forms of private capital inflows, and is expected to remain the main source of private capital to developing countries.[6] As the world economy strengthens, FDI flows are expected to rebound, with emerging markets capturing a growing share of global FDI.

Private capital and FDI into developing countries

Net private capital flows to developing countries—FDI, portfolio equity, and debt—grew rapidly from 2003 until the first half of 2008, peaking at $1.2 trillion in 2007 (table 1.2). FDI accounted for the lion's share of net private capital flows to developing countries during this decade (figure 1.1 and annex 2).

The increase in FDI to developing countries up until 2007 mirrored global trends in FDI flows (figure 1.2), surging on the back of strong global macroeconomic performance, high corporate profits, financial liquidity and lower credit

Table 1.2 Net private capital inflows to developing countries, 2001-2008
$ billion

	2001	2002	2003	2004	2005	2006	2007	2008[e]
Net private and official inflows	224.2	162.4	258.6	370.7	498.7	668.3	1157.7	727.3
Net private inflows	197.3	156.8	269.1	396.5	569.7	739.2	1157.5	706.9
Net equity inflows	172.3	161.5	181	254.7	347.2	462.7	658.6	599
Net FDI inflows	166	152.5	155.5	216	279.1	358.4	520	583
Net portfolio equity inflows	6.3	9	25.5	38.7	68.1	104.3	138.6	15.7
Net debt flows	51.9	0.9	77.6	116	151.5	205.6	499.1	128.3
Official creditors	26.9	5.6	-10.5	-25.8	-71	-70.9	0.2	20.4
Private creditors	25	-4.7	88.1	141.8	222.5	276.5	498.9	107.9

Source: World Bank 2009.
[e] *Estimate*

spreads, booming stock markets and, more recently, rising commodity prices.

Besides riding on global FDI trends, developing countries have also become more attractive investment destinations, given their growing weight on the global stage, investment opportunities, improved macroeconomic fundamentals, increased openness to foreign investment and improving overall business environment. Over the 1990s, on average, the emerging world absorbed a quarter of global FDI flows (compared with 12 percent in the second half of the 1980s); that share increased to 29 percent during 2000–2009, and reached a record 45 percent in 2009 (figure 1.2). Other projections even expect that, for the first time, the emerging world will absorb more than half of global FDI in 2009.[7]

The geographical distribution of FDI flows to the developing world, however, is uneven. Four countries—the BRICs—have together absorbed 46 percent of FDI flows into all emerging markets during 2000–2008, and 51 percent in 2008 alone. This concentration mirrors the economic weight of these countries in the developing world, and they are expected to remain the focus of foreign investment flows to emerging markets going forward.

By sector, the distribution of FDI to developing countries is also uneven, mirroring global trends. The service sector accounts for just over two thirds of the stock of FDI in emerging markets (mostly in financial services), while the manufacturing and primary sectors account for a quarter and 6 percent, respectively.[8]

FIGURE 1.1 NET PRIVATE CAPITAL INFLOWS TO DEVELOPING REGIONS, 2005-2008
$ billion

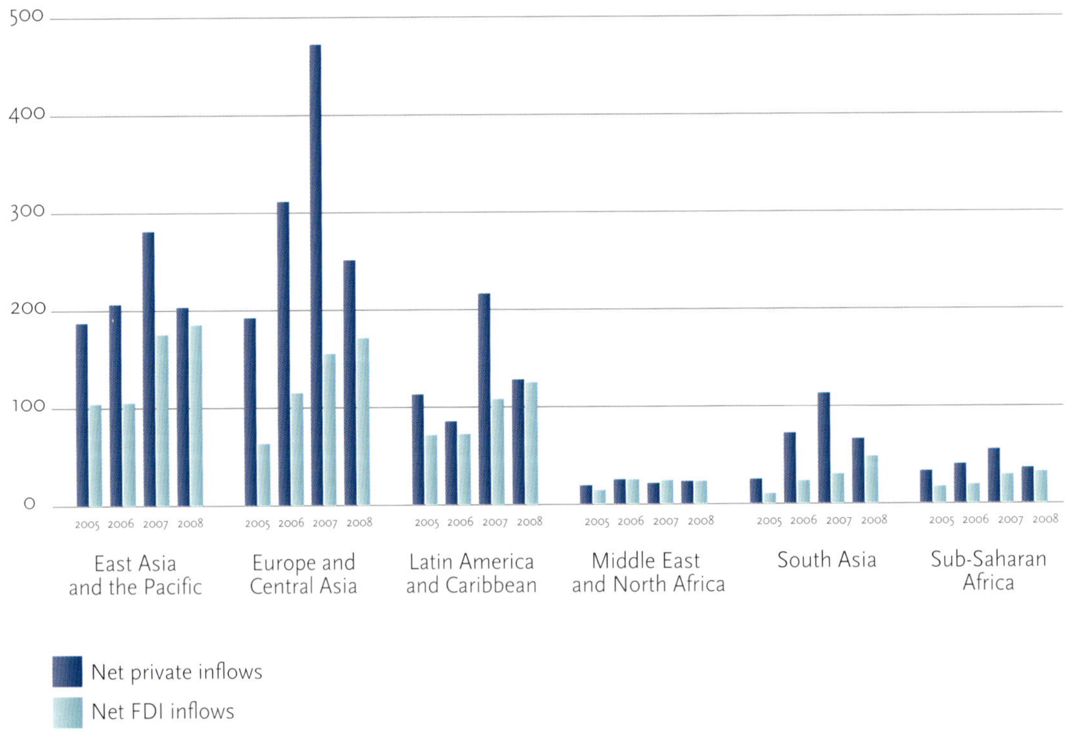

Source: World Bank 2009 (see also annex 2).
Note: 2008 figures based on staff estimates.

Developing countries as a source of FDI

Over the past few years, MNEs headquartered in emerging markets have established themselves as significant overseas investors, expanding in both industrialized and other developing countries. The share of developing countries in global FDI outflows increased from 1.4 percent in 2000 to 10.8 percent in 2008. Starting from a low base, the growth of outward FDI from the developing world began to accelerate in 2003 in tandem with global FDI flows. Between 2003 and 2008, FDI outflows from developing countries increased more than eight fold, reaching an estimated $198 billion in 2008 (figure 1.3). As is the case with inward FDI, outward FDI from emerging markets is also sourced from a few countries, the BRICs, which together accounted for 64 percent of emerging market outflows during 2000-2008 (figure 1.3), and 73 percent in 2008 alone. In 2008 FDI outflows from the developing world were led by China ($53.5 billion), the Russian Federation ($52.6 billion), Brazil ($20.5 billion), and India ($17.7 billion) (box 1.1). On a smaller scale, other developing countries have also emerged as significant foreign investors: for example, South Africa's outward FDI totaled $10.5 billion in 2006 and 2007, before turning negative in 2008 with a net divestment of $3.5 billion.

Investors from emerging markets often have a shorter history of investing abroad than those from industrialized countries, and their investments tend to be concentrated in countries in the same region, often in those with close cultural links. Yet a growing number of these emerging MNEs are venturing further afield in search of new markets and resources. India's FDI stock into emerging markets, for example, used to be concentrated in Asia, which accounted for a 75 percent share in the mid 1990s. By 2007, Asia's dominant position had eroded to just 39 percent, as Indian MNEs ventured into Africa

FIGURE 1.2 GLOBAL NET FDI INFLOWS, 1986-2009

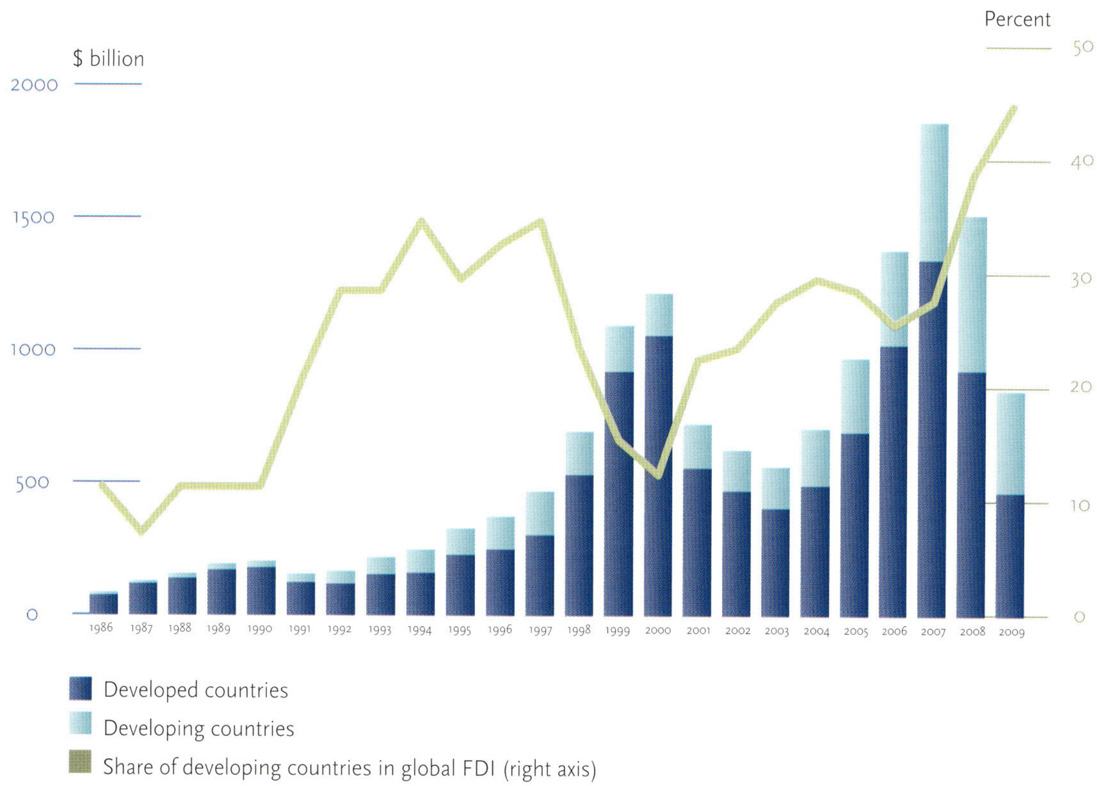

Source: World Bank 2009, and latest revised estimates (see also annex 1).
Note: 2008 figures based on staff estimates. 2009 figures based on forecasts.

(which accounted for 34 percent), Eastern Europe and the Commonwealth of Independent States (14 percent) and Latin America (13 percent). In China's case, Asia (including Hong Kong SAR, China) was the largest destination of its cumulative FDI outflows, accounting for 80 percent of the total in 2003—although a portion of Chinese FDI into Hong Kong SAR, China was invested back into China. By 2007 that share had declined to 67 percent, while Africa's share rose from 1.4 percent in 2003 to 4 percent in 2007.[9] Brazil's FDI stock in emerging markets is concentrated in Latin America, with Argentina and Uruguay accounting for over half the total.[10] Recently, however, its largest extractive MNEs have been investing in Africa.[11]

The growth of FDI from developing countries has been propelled by several factors.[12] First, developing countries are accounting for a growing share of the world GDP—from 17 percent in 1990 to 23 percent in 2007—and are consistently outpacing the industrialized world in terms of growth. Companies based there, having honed their

Box 1.1 Recent trends in FDI from the BRICs

The BRICs saw their combined outward FDI flows skyrocket from $29.6 billion in 2005 to $144.3 billion in 2008 (figure 1.3). In 2008, the BRICs together accounted for 73 percent of emerging market FDI outflows.

FDI from the BRICs received a major boost from the adoption in the early part of this decade of China's "go global" policy, aimed at inducing domestic enterprises to invest globally. China's FDI is concentrated in the services sector (70 percent),* followed by mining/oil (13 percent) and manufacturing (8 percent). Chinese FDI is carried out mostly by state-owned enterprises, which enables them to overcome financial constraints when investing abroad.

Indian outward FDI is also a relatively recent phenomenon, having increased from negligible levels in the middle of this decade to nearly $18 billion in 2008. Carried out mostly by publicly listed private-sector firms, Indian FDI is distributed across a range of sectors, such as steel and pharmaceuticals, information technology and business services. One notable exception is the energy sector, in which most Indian FDI has been carried out by the state-owned Oil and Natural Gas Corporation Ltd., the largest multinational in India (ranked according to size of foreign assets), through its subsidiary ONGC Videsh Ltd. Brazilian FDI increased from low levels in the middle of this decade to $21 billion in 2008. About half of the largest Brazilian MNEs focus on Latin America, where Brazil is the top investor in several countries. By sector, Brazil's FDI position is concentrated in financial services, followed by manufacturing of industrial products. Its largest MNEs, however, are concentrated in the natural resource sector. Most of Brazil's MNEs are private companies.

The Russian Federation has been viewing outward FDI more favorably in recent years. Russian FDI abroad more than quadrupled between 2005 and 2008, with the largest MNEs concentrated in metals and oil and gas. The majority of these companies are privately owned, but a number of them (e.g. Gazprom) are controlled by the state. Most FDI goes to countries in the same region, especially the Commonwealth of Independent States. When investing abroad, Russian MNEs seek to access foreign markets, natural resources and new technologies and knowhow. Russian oil and gas companies seek to engage in downstream integration via the establishment or acquisition of processing, storage and distribution facilities.

* *This includes investments channeled through tax havens.*

Sources: Davies (2009); Athreye Suma and Sandeep Kapur (2009); Indian School of Business and Vale Columbia Center on Sustainable International Investment (2009); Fundação Dom Cabral (FDC) and Vale Columbia Center on Sustainable International Investment (2007); Deloitte (2008); Moscow School of Management Skolkovo and Vale Columbia Center on Sustainable International Investment (2008); Skolkovo Institute for Emerging Market Studies (2009).

FIGURE 1.3 NET FDI OUTFLOWS FROM DEVELOPING COUNTRIES 2000-2008

$ billion

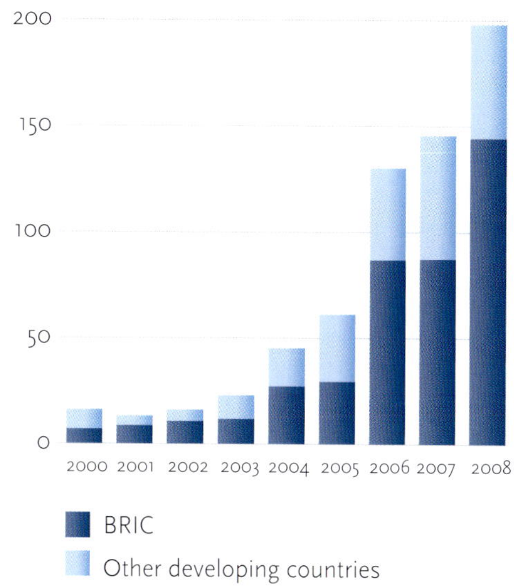

Source: World Bank 2009, and latest revised estimates.

competitiveness in their home markets and through international trade, are seeking to reach new markets and resources through FDI. In many developing countries, companies have reached a "take off" stage, a critical mass in terms of size, with enough resources to become global players.[13] Increasingly relaxed regulations on outward investment and removal of foreign exchange controls, as well as general encouragement by their own governments,[14] have facilitated the process of investing overseas.

The impact of the crisis on FDI

The financial crisis has severely curtailed private capital flows to developing countries, reversing the upward trends observed over the past few years. Yet FDI flows to emerging markets are proving resilient, and rebounds are anticipated in 2010.

Net private capital inflows to developing countries contracted by almost 40 percent by the end of 2008 to $707 billion (4.4 percent of developing-country GDP), (table 1.2). All developing regions, except the Middle East and North Africa, faced declines (figure 1.1), but emerging markets in Europe and Central Asia suffered the most from the financial crisis, accounting for 50 percent of the decline in capital flows to all developing countries. Net portfolio equity flows plummeted by 90 percent, while private debt flows contracted by 76 percent. The situation worsened in 2009 with another decline of net private capital flows to developing countries, projected to sink to $363 billion.

FDI has been more resilient than other forms of private capital, however. Despite the reduction in global FDI flows (box 1.2), foreign direct investment into the developing world continued to increase in 2008 (table 1.2). An additional $63 billion of FDI flowed into emerging markets in that year, equivalent to 3.5 percent of their combined GDP. The largest increase was registered in South Asia (with FDI flows to India rising by more than 50 percent), followed by Latin America and Sub-Saharan Africa. Nearly all developing regions received record levels of FDI inflows in 2008. The high commodity prices that persisted through at least the first half of that year continued to support investment in resource-rich developing countries, such as Brazil, Chile, Indonesia and Peru (annex 2).

FDI flows to emerging markets started slowing during the second half of 2008. In the first quarter of 2009, cross-border M&A in the developing world (mostly by developed-country MNEs) declined to $16 billion, compared with more than $30 billion in the previous two years. (FDI through cross-border M&As typically accounts for about 30 percent of all FDI flows into developing countries[15]). In 2009, tight credit conditions, weak global demand and low profitability owing to the recession are certain to limit the ability and willingness of MNEs to expand in the developing world. The World Bank projects FDI flows into developing countries to decline by 34 percent to $385 billion in 2009. Yet, FDI flows to developing countries remained more resilient than flows into industrialized countries in 2009 (where the World Bank estimates FDI inflows shrank by 50 percent).

The financial crisis also put a break on the growth in FDI flows from emerging markets. Estimates show that FDI outflows from developing countries increased in 2008 (figure 1.3), but are expected to decline in 2009. In Brazil, FDI outflows declined by 87 percent during the first five months of 2009.[16] In India, FDI outflows contracted by 14 percent in the first half of 2009[17], compared with the corresponding period in 2008. The OECD forecasts M&A spending—an early indicator of trends in FDI—by Brazil, China, India, Indonesia, the Russian Federation and South Africa to decline by over 80 percent to $21 billion in 2009 (down from $120 billion in 2008).[18]

Like their developed country counterparts, many MNEs from emerging markets faced financial difficulties during

Box 1.2 Impact of the Crisis on Global FDI

The financial crisis had a profound impact on FDI, with global flows declining by about 19 percent to just over $1.5 trillion in 2008, according to the World Bank. FDI to industrialized countries, which account for the bulk of global FDI, shrank to $927 billion from $1.3 trillion in 2007. Underscoring those trends was a fall in cross-border mergers and acquisitions, the value of which decreased sharply in 2008 and fell by 35 percent in the first half of 2009. MNEs also accelerated their repatriation of profits, opting against reinvestment, which would have counted towards the overall FDI figures. Divestment also accelerated, as troubled financial institutions raised capital by selling their overseas assets, usually to local companies.

The decline in global FDI flows took place via several channels. First, tighter credit affected the ability of MNEs to finance their projects abroad. Second, the economic recession hit corporate earnings, and hence their ability to finance expansions through reinvesting their own profits declined. Third, the recession led many MNEs to reduce or postpone their global expansion plans, and even divest from existing operations. FDI in certain sectors, such as financial services, the automotive industry, construction, building materials, intermediate goods and some consumer goods, have been amongst the most affected by the crisis.

Global FDI flows are expected to further contract in 2009. The World Bank estimates FDI flows worldwide to drop to $850 billion, with inflows to developed countries declining again to $466 billion. This is corroborated by other forecasts: UNCTAD projects global flows to shrink by as much as 47 percent in 2009, and OECD forecasts FDI flows into its 30 members (mostly industrialized countries) to decline to around $500 billion in 2009 from over $1 trillion in 2008.

Sources: World Bank 2009; UNCTAD 2009d; OECD press release, June 24, 2009.

the crisis. Prior to the financial crisis, a growing number of MNEs based in developing countries enjoyed access to international debt markets for the financing they needed to invest overseas.[19] The credit crunch, liquidity constraints, declining profitably and general economic uncertainty all affected their ability to finance new investments abroad through that route. Moreover, the global recession and commodity price decline from last year's all-time high curtailed revenues and profits. The decline in FDI outflows from developing countries, however, may well be relatively less severe than in the outflows from developed countries, as emerging MNEs may turn to domestic financial markets, generally better shielded from the impact of the crisis than international ones, to raise capital. Even before the crisis, China's state-owned MNEs were relying on state-owned domestic banks rather than foreign financial markets to finance their investment projects overseas, and will continue doing so.

Outlook for foreign direct investment

In spite of the severe impact of the crisis on FDI in 2009, the picture emerging for 2010 is cautiously optimistic, with global FDI expected to start recovering in line with the global economy.[20] The World Bank projects FDI flows to developing countries to bounce back, reaching $440 billion in 2010—below the record levels registered in 2007 and 2008, but higher than the 2006 FDI inflows.

The picture for FDI flows from developing countries is also optimistic, as MNEs based in emerging markets are expected to continue to shape the growth and pattern of global FDI in the future. China, despite the crisis, is renewing its efforts to encourage outward FDI as part of its "going global" strategy by relaxing foreign exchange restrictions, allowing domestic companies to borrow at home in foreign currency from a variety of sources, and easing regulatory procedures for outward investment.[21]

Historically, FDI flows have contracted during downturns, but these reductions tend to be short lived. Longer-term trends in FDI are shaped by corporate strategies that emphasize establishing a presence in a range of countries to serve local markets, integrating supply chains located in different countries, accessing natural resources, knowhow and skills, and brand acquisition. Combined with the continued openness to FDI and the dismantling of business obstacles, all of these factors point to a continued upward trend in FDI flows in the longer term.

Corporate Perspectives on Foreign Direct Investment

During the second quarter of 2009 MIGA commissioned a set of surveys of executives from MNEs to gauge their views on future investments in emerging markets; how political risks feature amongst the concerns and factors that constrain their investment plans; and the mechanisms used to mitigate political risk concerns (annexes 3 and 4 for details on these surveys). A survey of global investors was undertaken by the Economist Intelligence Unit on behalf of MIGA (the MIGA-EIU Political Risk Survey 2009, hereinafter referred to as the global survey). Another survey of investors based in BRIC countries was undertaken by the Vale Columbia Center on Sustainable International Investment along the same lines (the MIGA-VCC Political Risk Survey in the BRICs, hereinafter the BRIC survey). The following section summarizes the views of respondents with regards to cross-border investment plans in the short and medium terms. Investors' views on political risk are summarized in chapter 2.

Foreign Direct Investment Plans

As discussed above, the global financial crisis resulted in a decline in FDI into emerging markets in 2009. However, this decline appears to be more related to the tightening of financial markets—which has made funding scarcer and more expensive—than to investors' reassessment of the long-term business rationale for investing in emerging markets.

The global survey suggests that investors have maintained a positive outlook for FDI in general. Around 40 percent of them expect their firms to increase foreign investment this year, and a further 20 percent expect investment plans to remain in line with 2008. Around 65 percent of investors surveyed expect their foreign investment to increase over the next three years (figure 1.4). These figures suggest that investors do not anticipate the global financial and economic turmoil to affect their investment prospects for long. This is in line with macroeconomic projections (presented in the section above) expecting global FDI to start rebounding in 2010.

Investments in the short term will likely continue to be unevenly affected in different sectors (figure 1.5). Having faced a substantial drop in the price of commodities, almost half the surveyed investors in primary industries expect their foreign investments to decrease this year, in many cases by more than 20 percent when compared to 2008. In contrast, more than 60 percent of investors in other sectors, such as the financial industry, services and manufacturing, plan to increase or at least maintain foreign investments this year. In the next three years, however, a higher proportion of investors across all sectors expect to increase their foreign investments. This suggests that investors continue to maintain a positive outlook on business ventures in foreign markets.

Figure 1.4 Changes in foreign investment plans

Percent of respondents

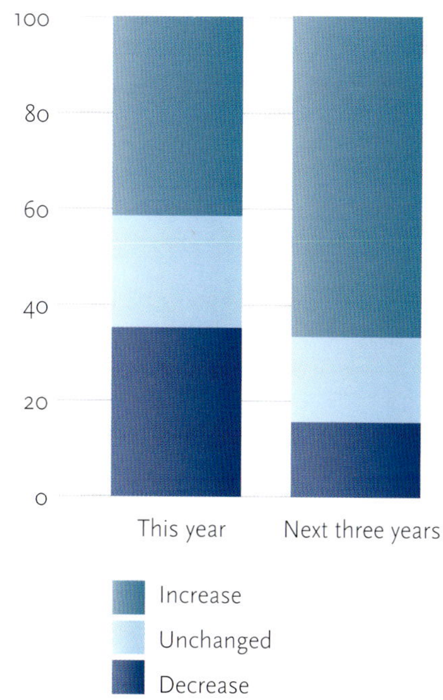

How do you expect your planned investments abroad to change this year compared with last year, and over the next three years compared with the previous three years?

Source: MIGA-EIU Political Risk Survey 2009.

Investment Intentions to Emerging Markets

Besides expecting their foreign investments to pick up relatively quickly, respondents of the global survey remain optimistic about economic prospects in emerging markets. In fact, 43 percent of respondents expect their firms to redirect investments away from developed markets and into developing ones over the next three years, confirming a robust interest in emerging market destinations (figure 1.6).[22] Investors in the manufacturing sector are the keenest to redirect their existing investments to emerging markets over the next three years, while 39 percent expect to do so this year. Companies from the United States and the United Kingdom show a higher propensity than investors from other countries to make that shift over the coming year—35 percent and 37 percent, respectively.

The BRICs are poised to continue receiving the lion's share of FDI into emerging markets (figure 1.7). Almost

60 percent of the investors surveyed are already present in China, and almost half are present in India. Investments in the Russian Federation and Brazil are less prevalent, with 40 percent and 39 percent of respondents having a presence there. Other investment destinations trail behind: Poland (21 percent), Mexico (16 percent), South Africa (14 percent) and Turkey (14 percent). Investors' responses correspond closely to country rankings by actual FDI inflows.

Outside the BRICs, Turkey and South Africa appear to attract increasing interest over the next three years, whereas Poland and Mexico—which have been hit hard by the global economic downturn—slip back. Among the investors surveyed, there is a noticeable decline in the relative attractiveness of Eastern European economies. This could reflect, among other things, investors' concerns over the impact of the global financial crisis on these countries at the time of the survey.

The survey highlights that FDI remains regional to some degree. Latin American destinations, for example, still feature more prominently in investments from US firms than in those from other regions—25 percent compared to an average of 19 percent for all investors—even though

Figure 1.5 Changes in foreign investment plans by sector

Percent of respondents

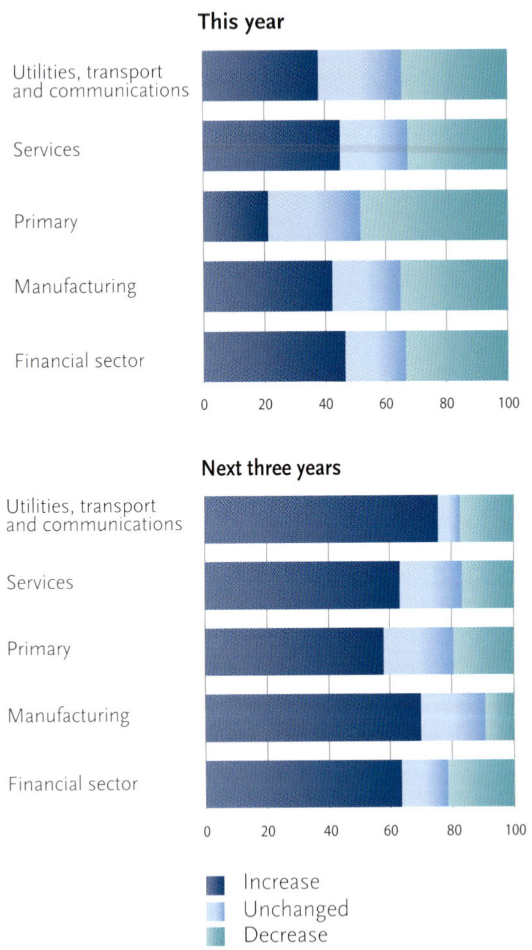

How do you expect your company's planned investments abroad to change this year compared with last year and over the next three years compared with the previous three years?

Source: MIGA-EIU Political Risk Survey 2009.

Figure 1.6 Changes in foreign investment plans by destination

Percent of respondents

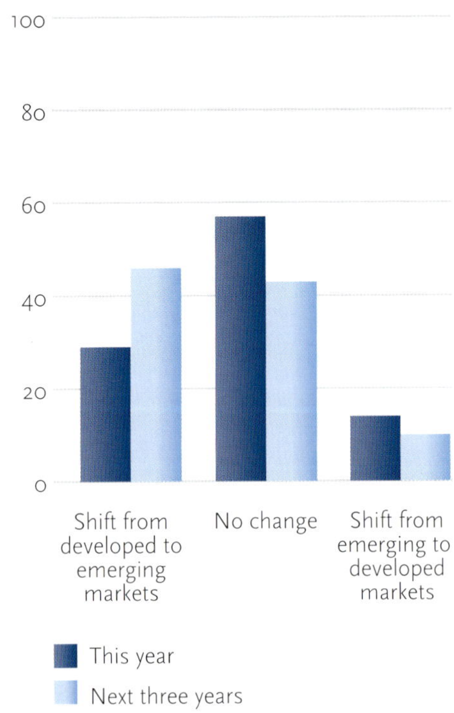

Do you expect your company to shift its foreign investments from emerging to developed markets, or vice versa?

Source: MIGA-EIU Political Risk Survey 2009.

the share of European investment in that region has been rising. Likewise, investors from Western Europe dominate investment into Eastern Europe, which is a top investment destination for a third of Western European investors, compared to 26 percent on average. The survey findings suggest that this pattern is unlikely to change over the next three years.

Figure 1.7 Top ten investment destinations

Percent of respondents

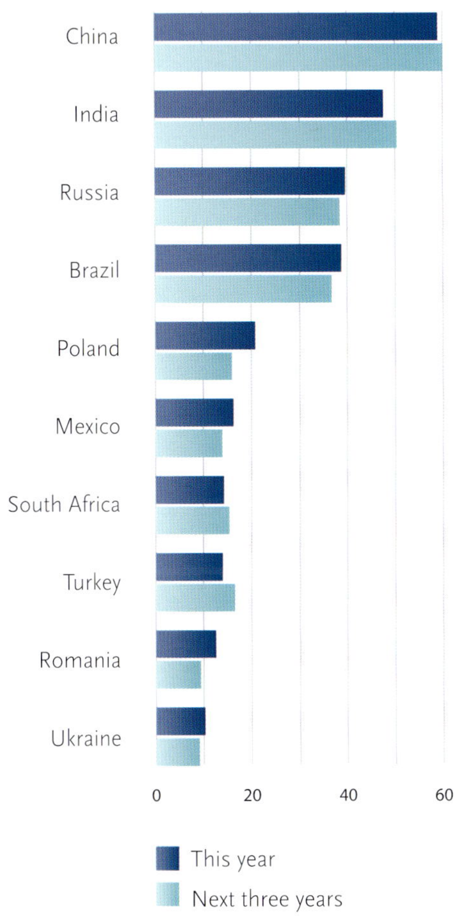

What are the five main emerging market destinations for your company's direct investments abroad today?

And, in what five emerging markets does your company plan the highest level of new investment over the next three years?

Source: MIGA-EIU Political Risk Survey 2009.
Note: Percentages add up to more than 100 percent due to multiple selections.

Figure 1.8 Changes in foreign investment plans by source

Percent of respondents

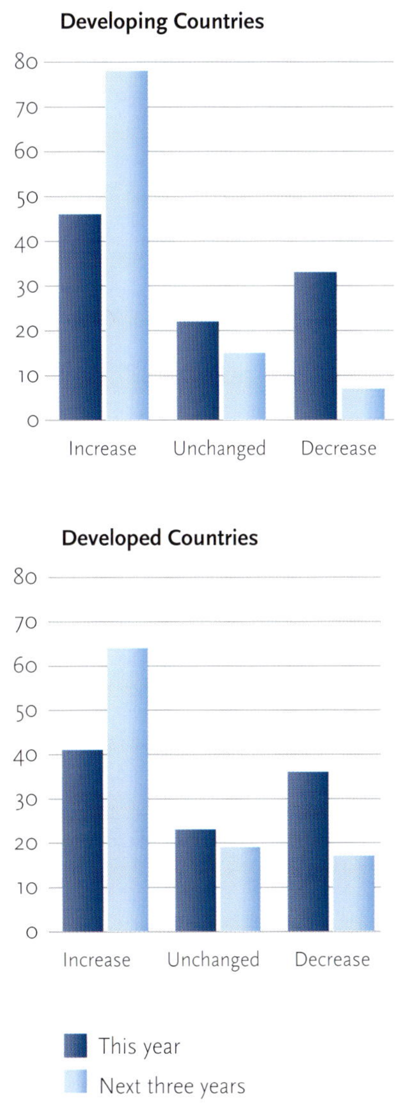

How do you expect your company's planned investments abroad to change this year compared with last year and over the next three years compared with the previous three years?

Source: MIGA-EIU Political Risk Survey 2009.

Figure 1.9 Foreign investment plans of investors from the BRICs

Percent of respondents

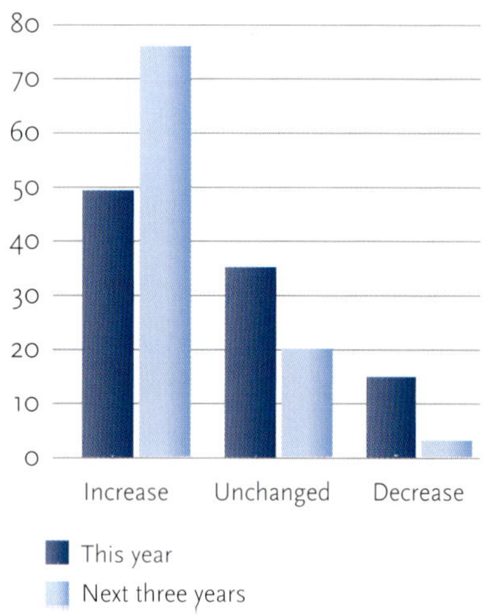

How do you expect your company's planned investments abroad to change this year compared with last year and over the next three years compared with the previous three years?

Source: MIGA-VCC Political Risk Survey in the BRICs 2009.

Investors from Emerging Markets and FDI

The emerging-market MNEs surveyed appeared to be more bullish than their counterparts in developed countries regarding their investment plans. A higher proportion of them expected their investments overseas to increase or remain the same over the next year than investors from the developed world. The gap in investment intentions between emerging-market investors and those from developed countries was even more pronounced over the medium term: some 80 percent of emerging market respondents planned to increase investment over the next three years, compared with just over 60 percent of developed country respondents (figure 1.8).

The BRIC survey confirms the optimism of emerging-market investors.[23] Although a third of the BRIC respondents did not plan any changes in their companies' investment plans this year (figure 1.9), 49 percent intended to increase investments moderately or substantially (55 percent of the Chinese MNEs, half of the Brazilian MNEs and 48 percent of the Indian MNEs). These intentions intensified over the next three years, with some three quarters of respondents planning a substantial or moderate increase in FDI. Chinese investors appeared the most bullish, while Russian respondents were the most cautious, with only 30 percent or so expecting to increase investments this year and over the next three years. While the crisis has dampened the growth of FDI outflows from developing countries this year, the BRIC survey findings suggest this may be short lived—at least for Chinese, Indian and Brazilian investors.

***

Investor surveys suggest robust optimism about investment prospects in developing countries over the next three years, sustained by signs that a recovery of the global economy is underway. A more pessimistic economic scenario cannot yet be excluded, however, and risks of reversal persist. Persistent economic imbalances could become more apparent as emergency policy measures begin to wane, and unsustainable debt positions have to be unwound. Renewed concerns regarding the sustainability of the rebound would affect private capital flows, including FDI. For now, the expected growth rebound in emerging markets, while uneven, appears strong enough to sustain survey respondents' investment intentions.

Chapter One —Endnotes

1 *Foreign direct investment is defined as an investment involving a long term relationship and reflecting a lasting interest and control by a resident entity in one economy in an enterprise resident in an economy other than that of the foreign direct investor. It comprises equity investment, reinvested earnings and intra-company loans.*

2 *The surveys did not include respondents representing sovereign and private equity funds. Investor views presented in this report cover MNEs' perspectives only.*

3 *As of September 25, 2009, 12 out of 42 emerging market sovereigns had a negative outlook, compared with 16 out of 43 six months ago. Standard and Poor's (2009).*

4 *All data in this chapter are from World Bank (2009), unless otherwise specified.*

5 *For a broader discussion of the financial crisis and its impact on the world economy, see World Bank (2009).*

6 *The resilience of FDI flows—comprising for statistical purposes of equity investment, reinvested earnings and intra-company loans—can be traced primarily to its equity component. The volatility of the reinvested earnings and intra-company loans can be quite significant, especially at times of economic distress (World Bank, 2009, Box 2.2).*

7 *MIGA-EIU Political Risk Survey (2009) and Kekic (2009).*

8 *UNCTAD (2009d), annex table A.I.4*

9 *Cheng and Ma (2007) and Davies (2009).*

10 *Lima and de Barros (2009). The data for Brazil exclude tax havens.*

11 *"Brazil's Vale starts $1.3 billion coal project in Africa", MarketWatch, March 28, 2009; "Petrobras to invest $2 billion in Nigerian oil", Engineering News, February 25, 2009.*

12 *For a discussion of the drivers of FDI from developing countries, see World Bank (2006).*

13 *The Financial Times Global 500 list, which ranks companies by market capitalization, showed that firms from developing countries accounted for 17 percent of the world's leading companies in 2008, up from minuscule levels a few years ago. For banking and finance, which in 2008 became the leading sector for FDI worldwide, some 20 percent of The Banker's largest 1,000 banks and more than one-third of the top 20 banks were from developing countries.*

14 *Luo, Xue and Han (2009).*

15 *World Bank (2009).*

16 *Lima and de Barros (2009).*

17 *Reserve Bank of India (2009).*

18 *OECD (2009).*

19 *World Bank (2009).*

20 *See UNCTAD (2009d) and MIGA-EIU Political Risk Survey (2009).*

21 *Davies (2009).*

22 *Only one in ten investors surveyed is considering the reverse over the next three years; most of these firms are in the primary or financial sectors and are headquartered in North America or Western Europe.*

23 *See annex 4 for details on the MIGA-VCC Political Risk Survey in the BRICs.*

CHAPTER TWO

THE CHALLENGE OF POLITICAL RISK

Overview

As signs of economic recovery in the aftermath of the most severe crisis in the post war era emerge (chapter 1), concerns over political risk continue to loom large. While the link between FDI and political risk is not straightforward, investors repeatedly rank political perils amongst their main concerns when venturing abroad. Understanding investors' current outlook on both risks and opportunities in developing countries is essential to shed some light on how the PRI industry can help mitigate concerns over political risks.[1]

The global economic downturn, by straining government budgets, putting pressure on exchange rates and bringing political and social tensions to the fore, has exacerbated specific political risks in the most vulnerable investment destinations, but does not appear to have led to a reassessment of political risk in all emerging markets. For example, concerns that government may be tempted to impose transfer and convertibility restrictions have emerged in highly leveraged countries where the financial crisis has severely undermined liquidity and led to high spreads. With unemployment on the rise, declining remittances and pressure on social programs due to shrinking government revenues, the risk of civil unrest has become more pronounced in some countries. Budgetary pressures and stimulus packages have also raised concerns about the ability of some governments and state-owned entities to fulfill their contractual obligations and honor their sovereign guaranties. These risks, however, have so far not materialized on a large scale, and are less likely to do so as the effects of the crisis abate.

While corporate investors appear sanguine about investment prospects, in particular in emerging markets (chapter 1), political risk remains a major concern in the medium term, according to surveys of MNEs conducted for this report. Concerns over some longer-term political risks are likely to persist, even if some of the perils directly related to the fallout of the crisis recede as the global economy gradually recovers. The growing salience of political risk concerns, a trend that predates the onset of the global crisis, can partly be attributed to the increasing weight of developing countries—typically regarded as riskier destinations than industrialized ones—as foreign investment recipients. Over the past few years, the revival of resource nationalism in some countries, as well as contract renegotiations, have also weighed on political risk perceptions in extractive industries. Terrorist attacks have highlighted the emergence of new threats. And while political risk was thought to be a preoccupation primarily for investors from industrialized countries, it now appears to be a top concern for investors from the main emerging markets as well, as they venture further away from familiar business destinations.

Robust appetite for investment into emerging markets, combined with the persisting salience of political risks going forward, suggest a sustained need to manage and mitigate these risks. Yet most investors, both South- and North-based, appear to rely primarily on their own risk management capacity (even though a sizable minority judges that capacity as poor) and on informal mitigation mechanisms, such as engaging host governments and local communities, to evaluate and manage political risk. The proportion of respondents using contractual political risk management products such as PRI when investing in emerging markets is relatively small, which insurance industry statistics confirm (chapter 3). This suggests that most investors regard political risk in their main investment destinations as manageable. However, a much larger proportion of investors seek PRI when venturing into markets considered the riskiest, suggesting that PRI has a significant role to play protecting investors in transactions that are beyond their internal risk management capacity. The surveys also suggest investors' interest in PRI, with 40 percent of respondents in the global survey saying they will consider it going forward.

Political Risk, Foreign Direct Investment and Corporate Perceptions

What is Political Risk?

Broadly defined, political risk is the probability of disruption of the operations of MNEs by political forces or events,[2] whether they occur in host countries, home country, or result from changes in the international environment. In host countries, political risk is largely determined by uncertainty over the actions of governments and political institutions, but also of minority groups, such as separatist movements. In home countries, political risk may stem from political actions directly aimed at investment destinations, such as sanctions, or from policies that restrict outward investment.

For the purposes of the investor surveys conducted for this report, political risk was more specifically defined as breach of contract by governments, restrictions on currency transfer and convertibility, expropriation, political violence (war, civil disturbance and terrorism), non-honoring of government guarantees, adverse regulatory changes, and restrictions on FDI outflows in home countries. This definition includes risks that are not currently insurable by the PRI industry.

The insurance industry uses a narrower definition of political risk that focuses on actions that take place within host countries only. According to this definition, political risk is divided into (i) currency convertibility and transfer, (ii) expropriation, (iii) political violence, (iv) breach of contract by a host government, and (v) the non-honoring of sovereign financial obligations (box 3.2). Although there is a general consensus over these categories within the PRI industry, exact definitions vary among insurers.

Evolution of Political Risks

Although surveys suggest that investors are concerned about political risk when venturing abroad, the link between political risk and FDI is not straightforward (annex 5). More research is needed to determine the weight of political risk when compared to other factors that influence investment decisions, and clarify how the level of perceived risk influences FDI flows. The nature of political risk makes it difficult to predict and quantify, and concerns are primarily based on perceptions. These perceptions are influenced by broad geopolitical and economic trends, as well as local conditions.

The nature and perceptions of political risk have evolved over the past 30 years. The risk of expropriation was prominent in the 1970s, when MNEs found themselves at the core of public scrutiny, with their operations nationalized or controlled tightly. Especially in the area of natural resources and other industries deemed strategic by host country governments, MNEs found their autonomy waning.[3] Over that period, expropriation losses resulted primarily from outright confiscation of foreign assets. The number of foreign expropriations declined drastically in the 1980s,[4] however: while there were 423 cases of expropriation of foreign assets in the 1970s, that number dropped to 17 during 1980-1987 and to zero between 1987 and 1992.[5]

Over the same period, most emerging markets allocated foreign exchange via permits, and current and capital accounts controls were prevalent. This controlled foreign investors' ability to access and repatriate foreign exchange during balance of payments crises. As a result, a large number of transfer restriction claims occurred during the 1980s, triggered by the Latin American debt crisis and the subsequent fallout on the Philippines.

Transfer and expropriation risks appeared to ease significantly throughout the 1990s, as many countries began to liberalize their economies. Financial liberalization resulted in floating exchange rate regimes and the allocation of foreign exchange via market mechanisms through the banking sector, while capital controls were relaxed. These reforms eased the insurable risk of convertibility and transfer restrictions, but increased the uninsured risk of depreciation.

In the 1990s, the regulatory framework for FDI was characterized by increasing openness and a retreat of government intervention, as the benefits of foreign investment were deemed to exceed any adverse effects. Out of 1,097 changes in national FDI laws alone adopted between 1992 and 2000, 94 percent created a more favorable climate.[6] Many countries went beyond establishing an open environment for FDI by proactively seeking to attract such investment via incentives, targeted investment promotion programs and pro-active marketing. This has been complemented by greater efforts by many developing countries to reduce barriers to doing business.[7] In addition, the multiplication of bilateral investment treaties (BITs)[8] for the protection and promotion of FDI supported the trend towards greater openness and increasing FDI flows—globally and to developing countries. Investment also emerged as a focus of international agreements related to trade in goods and services, intellectual property rights and regional integration schemes.[9]

Although the trend toward reform and greater investment openness that gained force in the 1990s largely continues to-date,[10] concerns over political risk persist, as documented in a number of surveys (annex 5). In the global survey (annex 3), MNEs investing in developing countries rank political risk amongst their top three concerns more often than any other preoccupation, including macroeconomic stability and access to finance. A higher proportion of respondents expect political risk to be among their main investment constraints over the next three years (figure 2.1).

Ironically, the apparent resurgence of some political risks concerns over the past few years could be the result of greater openness to FDI, as the gradual dissolution of traditional barriers to investment may have amplified the relative salience of political risk among investor preoccupations. In addition, greater openness has contributed not only to an increase in global FDI, but also to a growing share flowing into developing countries (chapter 1). That emerging markets are perceived to be riskier destinations than industrialized countries is compounded by the number of investors expanding their business horizons by venturing into regions or countries for the first time.

In addition, MNEs based in developing countries have been investing growing amounts abroad (chapter 1). Some of that investment is in natural resources in countries beyond their regions of origin (e.g.

FIGURE 2.1 MAJOR CONSTRAINTS ON FOREIGN INVESTMENT IN EMERGING MARKETS
Percent of respondents

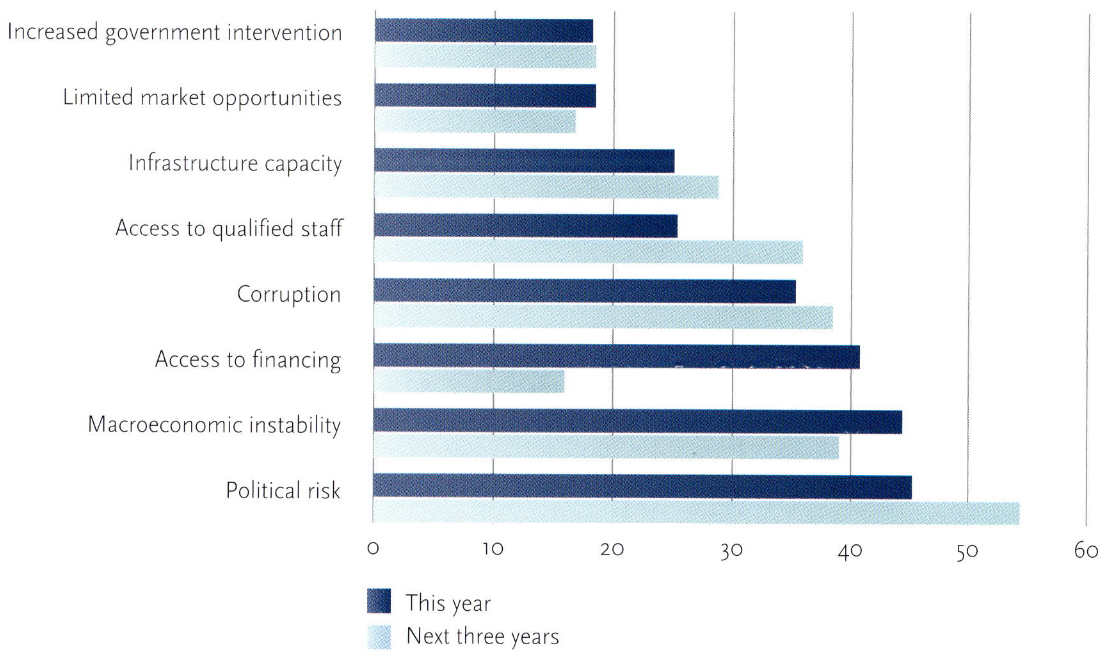

In your opinion, which of the following factors will pose the greatest constraint on investments by your company in emerging markets this year and over the next three years?

Source: MIGA-EIU Political Risk Survey 2009.
Note: Percentages add up to more than 100 percent due to multiple selections.

Brazil in Africa). Attention to political risk tends to be high during the first few years of operating in a new market, before sufficient familiarity and coping mechanisms are developed. As these enterprises spread their operations into new destinations in developing countries, they become more aware of political risk. This has contributed to the increase in demand for PRI from South-based investors (chapter 3).

Besides these general trends, the recent evolution of specific perils also contributed to a revival of political risk concerns that predates the global economic downturn.

Expropriation, breach of contract and non-honoring of government guarantees. Concerns over expropriation have reemerged over the past few years. The nature of expropriation, however, has evolved compared to the 1970s and 1980s. Outright nationalizations have become the exception rather than the norm. Changes in regulations or contractual agreements that undermine the financial viability of investments—as in Indonesia or Argentina in the late 1990s and early 2000s (chapter 3)—now dominate expropriation risks. Although the vast majority of changes in foreign investment regulations still go toward more openness, there are signs that FDI has been subjected to increasing scrutiny over the past few years.[11] The global survey confirms that more investors are concerned about breach of contract, non-honoring of government guarantees and adverse regulatory changes—which can result in investment loss—than outright expropriation. Breach of contract is the political risk of most concern to respondents, both this year and over the medium term. An increasing proportion of respondents are concerned about the risk of adverse regulatory changes going forward, with a third of them regarding it as a top concern in the next three years (figure 2.2).

Extractive industries are still particularly vulnerable to expropriation and breach of contract. The strategic nature of natural resources in host countries' economies, long

FIGURE 2.2 TYPES OF POLITICAL RISKS OF MOST CONCERN TO INVESTORS IN EMERGING MARKETS

Percent of respondents

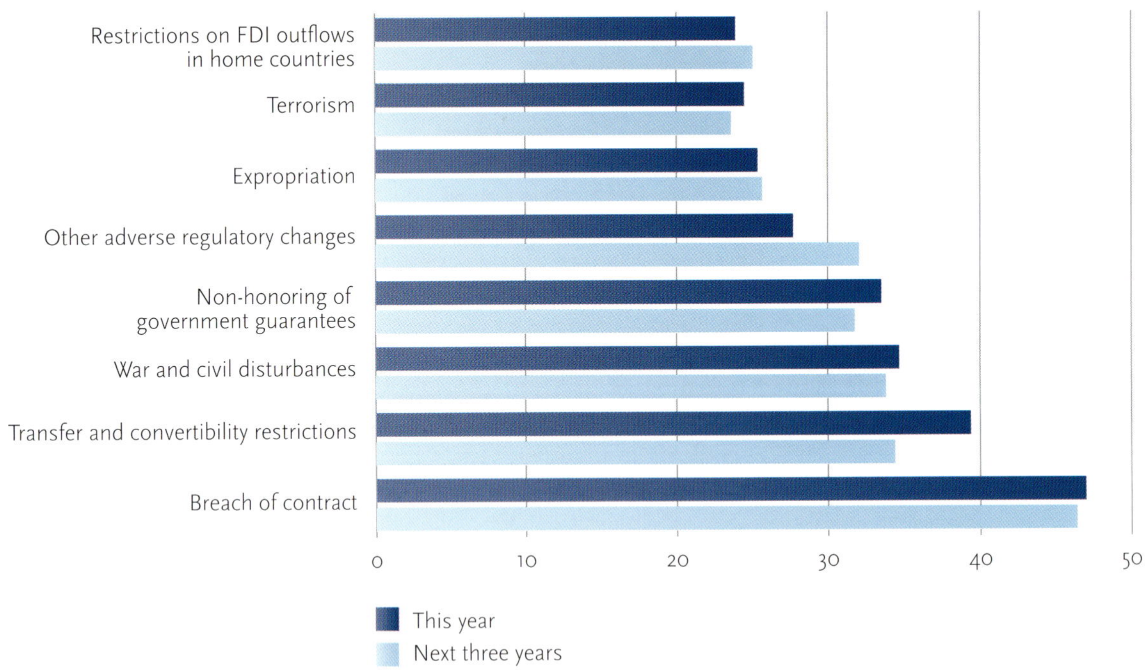

In your opinion, which types of political risk are of most concern to your company when investing in emerging markets?

Source: MIGA-EIU Political Risk Survey 2009.
Note: Percentages add up to more than 100 percent due to multiple selections.

investment horizons, scale and capital intensity also make these projects prone to uncertainty and possible government intervention. In a global environment of rising commodity prices, as was the case prior to the financial crisis, some governments renegotiated concession and royalty agreements struck with foreign investors a decade ago, when commodity markets were depressed.[12] Other governments motivated by nationalist political agendas have sought to reclaim ownership of the mining sector by nationalizing foreign owned assets. This apparent resurgence of "resource nationalism" has heightened perceptions of expropriation and associated risks in recent years.[13]

Indeed, the global survey confirms that investors operating in the primary sector—mostly in the extractive industries—are more concerned about political risks in general than in other sectors: 57 percent cite political risk as a major concern this year, compared with an average of 45 percent for all sectors. Of particular concern to investors are breach of contract and expropriation. Investors in the primary sectors worried more about the risk of breach of contract than in any other sector, with 54 percent citing it as a top risk. Similarly, over 45 percent of respondents from the primary sector also considered expropriation a top risk, compared to an average of 25 percent among all respondents.

Sub-sovereign authorities have also become an increasing source of risk for foreign investors—especially expropriation, breach of contract and non-honoring of guarantees—over the past few years. As emerging economies embrace decentralization, local authorities, such as provincial or municipal governments, are expected to take on increasing responsibilities in providing infrastructure services. In recent years, disputes have arisen in the power sector in countries where the sub-sovereign has not been able to fulfill its commitments, and central governments have been hesitant to take over these obligations.

Transfer and Convertibility. In spite of liberalization of exchange regimes and more prudent monetary policies, transfer and convertibility risks have not disappeared. In the last 10 years, several countries have restricted current or capital account transactions, or frozen foreign currency bank deposits to limit foreign exchange outflows. But foreign exchange restrictions now tend to be imposed for shorter durations, and scaled back as the economy re-balances. Nevertheless this risk is still prevalent, especially when financial crises strike. In the global survey, 39 percent of respondents cited it as one of their three main political risk concerns (figure 2.2).

Political Violence. Fresh worries over political violence have emerged in the past decade. The September 11 attacks highlighted the risk of terrorism. As terrorist attacks around the world continue to make headlines, risk perceptions are undiminished.[14] Threats stemming from separatist and extremist movements, civil unrest, as well as piracy and hijacking that threaten to disrupt supply chains, have also weighed on political risk perceptions. Respondents in the global survey ranked political violence (combining war, civil disturbance and terrorism) as their second main concern after breach of contract[15] (figure 2.2).

The preoccupations over political risk mentioned above are expected to outlive the current global downturn and persist over the medium term. In addition, the financial and economic turmoil itself has generated new concerns over political perils.

The Impact of the Financial Crisis on Political Risk Perceptions

The onset of the recent global financial crisis has intensified concerns over specific political risks in the most vulnerable countries. A comparison between the political risk ratings for the 126 emerging markets covered by the Economist Intelligence Unit's Risk Briefing between pre-crisis June 2008 and the ratings for June 2009 show a degradation of perceptions: the political risk score had increased for 52 countries (41 percent of the total number of emerging markets in Risk Briefing), remained unchanged for 49 countries (39 percent), and decreased for 25 countries (20 percent) over this period.[16]

The most significant deterioration of political risk perceptions between June 2008 and June 2009 was over Eastern Europe, followed by Latin America, developing Asia, Sub-Saharan Africa and Middle East and North Africa. This is also roughly the order of the comparative severity with which the global economic crisis has affected emerging market regions. Social unrest showed the highest increase among the various types of political risk in the Risk Briefing, followed by the related risk of violent demonstrations, and the imposition of capital account controls, all of which are closely related to the global financial and economic crisis.

With unemployment on the rise, declining remittances,[17] and fewer resources available to social programs due to shrinking government revenues,[18] many developing countries are exposed to a risk of social unrest. To date, however, the crisis has amplified—rather than created—unrest in countries where social relations were already fragile.[19] The risk of social unrest and political violence directly related to the current crisis is expected to ease gradually as economies recover.

In addition to possible social or political unrest, the global economic downturn has also exacerbated political risks arising from balance of payments shortfalls and revived the risk of transfer restrictions (box 2.1). The crisis has had an adverse impact on some countries' current account balances through shrinking international trade and the decline in commodity prices. The accumulation of foreign reserves has suffered from the impact as countries are drawing upon them to lessen the impact of the financial crisis.[20] Private sources of capital are also drying up, and developing countries are expected to face greatly curtailed access to external financing (chapter 1). The World Bank estimates the external financing gap for developing countries to be $352 billion in 2009 for a base case scenario.[21] International assistance, however, is helping cushion the impact of the crisis. Several developing countries have received financial support from multilateral institutions to help alleviate balance-of-payments difficulties.[22]

Investors surveyed for this report expect the risk of convertibility and transfer to recede over the next three years, with around a third citing it as concern in three years, compared to 39 percent this year. This could reflect optimism that the financial crisis will ease over this period. Concerns over this risk were concentrated in Eastern Europe and Central Asia for this year, where many markets relied heavily on foreign financing, and some have pegged foreign exchange regimes.

Budgetary pressures, due to slower economic growth, and priority on stimulus packages, could also weaken the ability of some governments and state-owned entities in developing countries to fulfill their contractual obligations and honor their sovereign guaranties. These pressures are particularly acute in countries where fiscal deficits are high compared to GDP. Between 2008 and 2009, Europe and Central Asia is expected to have the largest increase in fiscal deficit in relation to its economic size, followed by Sub-Saharan Africa.[23] Deteriorating fiscal positions raise the risk of payment defaults by sovereign (or sub-sovereign) and state-owned entities. Respondents in the global survey expect the risk of host governments failing to honor their guarantees to remain roughly the same over the medium term: 34 percent of respondents consider it as a main risk today, compared to 32 percent in three years (figure 2.2).

The financial crisis also gave rise to concerns that governments in both developed and developing countries may adopt policies to alleviate the effects of the crisis that might restrict outward FDI or discriminate against foreign investors.[24] Yet several reports tracking regulatory changes in investment since the onset of the crisis have found no general trend in that direction so far.[25]

Yet, the risks directly related to the fallout from global crisis have so far not materialized on a large scale, and they are likely to ease as economic recovery slowly takes hold. The global survey suggests that the global crisis has not led to a fundamental reassessment of political risks in the top FDI recipients in emerging markets: a majority of investors stated that the downturn itself had not affected their risk perceptions in their main investment destinations (35 percent considered the risk to be worse, however). As the BRICs dominate investment destinations (figure 1.7), this could reflect investor confidence in these countries' ability to weather a global crisis.

The global survey suggests that host countries' recent track records of political stability, rule of law and investor protection—rather than economic difficulties—are the main features influencing investors' perception of overall political risk. The investors surveyed were asked to provide their perceptions of political risk for the 40 largest emerging markets ranked according to the size of population. The ten countries most frequently identified by investors as the markets with the highest political risk included a number of countries that are at war or emerging from conflict, as well as others that have recently experienced acts of civil disturbance or where government decisions adversely affected foreign investors (annex 3).

Corporate Perceptions of Political Risk Management

A majority of survey respondents expected to ramp up their investments in emerging markets over the next three years, as highlighted in chapter 1. Combined with an increasing proportion of investors citing political risks as the top investment constraint over the medium term, this suggests a growing need to properly manage these risks.

Yet most respondents have so far relied on internal risk assessments and informal mitigation tools—such as engagement with host country governments or joint ventures with local companies—or have not mitigated political risks at all. Political risk insurance features as a niche product primarily used for projects and destinations considered the riskiest. Yet 40 percent of respondents in the global survey expect they will consider PRI going forward.

A majority of investors surveyed for this report were confident in their ability to appraise and manage political risks. But a significant minority was not: 24 percent of investors considered their ability to anticipate new political risks to be weak or non-existent (figure 2.3). Similarly, 29 percent of respondents regarded their ability to evaluate political risk mitigation strategies as weak or non-existent, and 23 percent admitted that their capabilities to implement those strategies were also poor. These findings suggest a sizable portion of investors may need assistance with assessing and managing political risks.

Box 2.1 Transfer and Convertibility Risk

Standard & Poor's (S&P), the rating agency, assigns transfer and convertibility (T&C) ratings that address the probability of such government interventions. During 2008, Standard & Poor's downgraded its T&C ratings on 13 countries, 12 of which are in the developing world (box figure). With the exception of countries affected by specific conflicts, these downgrades stem directly from the impact of the global financial crisis and imply an increased probability that host governments might intervene in their markets in ways that would be detrimental to the interests of foreign investors. According to rating agencies, the likelihood of such interventions appears to depend not only on macroeconomic factors, but also on political stability and governments' institutional strength. Indeed, all other things equal, a government committed to sustainable economic policies and with the authority to pursue them, would be in a better position to respond to the challenges posed by the financial crisis.

Most of the recent downgrades in T&C ratings are concentrated in Europe and Central Asia (ECA), where ratings on two out of three assessed countries were cut in the last year (box figure). According to S&P, the vulnerability of many countries in the ECA region stems from the characteristics of their financing structure, including large current account deficits, significant external public and/or private debt, and short-term maturities. Comparatively, many emerging economies in Latin America and Asia have manageable levels of external debt, and have successfully developed sizeable domestic capital markets, largely funded by private pension funds, which so far have provided relatively stable funding to local corporate borrowers.

Changes in T&C ratings during 2008

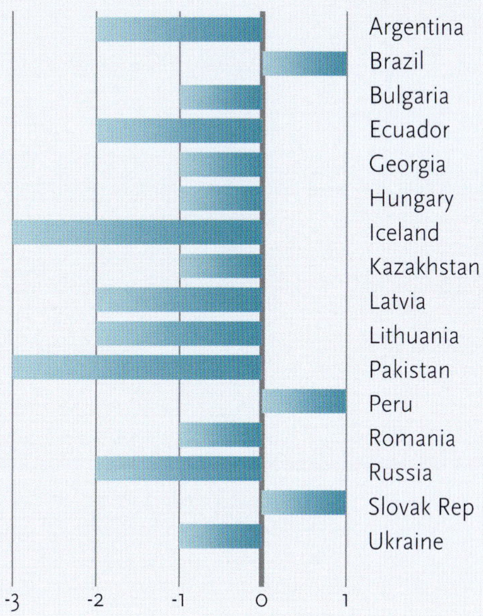

Source: Standard & Poor's
Note: Bars represent the change in number of notches in S&P's rating scale.

Most investors claimed that they manage political risks utilizing a wide range of mechanisms, and in many instances using more than one mitigation tool (figure 2.4). Most respondents relied on risk or scenario analysis to assess perils. A majority of respondents used informal tools, such as engagement with host country governments, as a way to mitigate political risks. Around a third of respondents managed risks through joint ventures with local partners, while a similar proportion engaged risk consultants.

A small proportion of respondents, on the other hand, used contractual risk mitigation such as credit default swaps (17 percent), or PRI (14 percent). This is broadly in line with PRI industry data indicating that new political risk insurance policies underwritten in 2008 by members of the largest insurance association covered around 10 percent of FDI flows to emerging markets (chapter 3).

The global crisis had a limited impact on desire to use risk-mitigating tools: the majority of investors (57 percent) reported that the crisis had not changed the attractiveness of these instruments one way or the other. A significant minority of respondents, however, found mitigation tools more attractive due to the downturn (19 percent).

About 6 percent of the investors reported that they do not mitigate political risk at all (figure 2.4). The most common reason cited by investors was that the level of political risk in destination countries was not high enough (less frequently cited reasons included the cost of mitigation and inadequacy of products). Yet many of these respondents had investments in countries with a relatively high degree of risk, which indicates a wide variance in risk perceptions and tolerance—or in investors' ability to assess political risk adequately.

While a similar proportion of investors across all sectors undertake risk analysis and engage with host country governments, the use of other mitigation techniques varied across industries (table 2.1). About half of the respondents operating in the primary sector, utilities, transport and communications mitigated risks through joint ventures with local partners, while only one third of respondents did so in the financial sector, manufacturing and services. Financial sector investors, however, were much more frequent users of formal risk mitigation mechanisms, such as credit default swaps and PRI.

Several factors influence investors' decisions to contract political risk insurance (box 2.2). The global investor survey confirms that the level of risk in host countries is a major determinant. Although only 14 percent of investors in the global survey reported using political risk insurance on average, 22 percent of companies investing in what they perceived to be high-risk countries turned to PRI. This suggests that investors are confident they can manage risks effectively in most destinations, and

Figure 2.3 Investors' capabilities in assessing and mitigating political risks

Percent of respondents

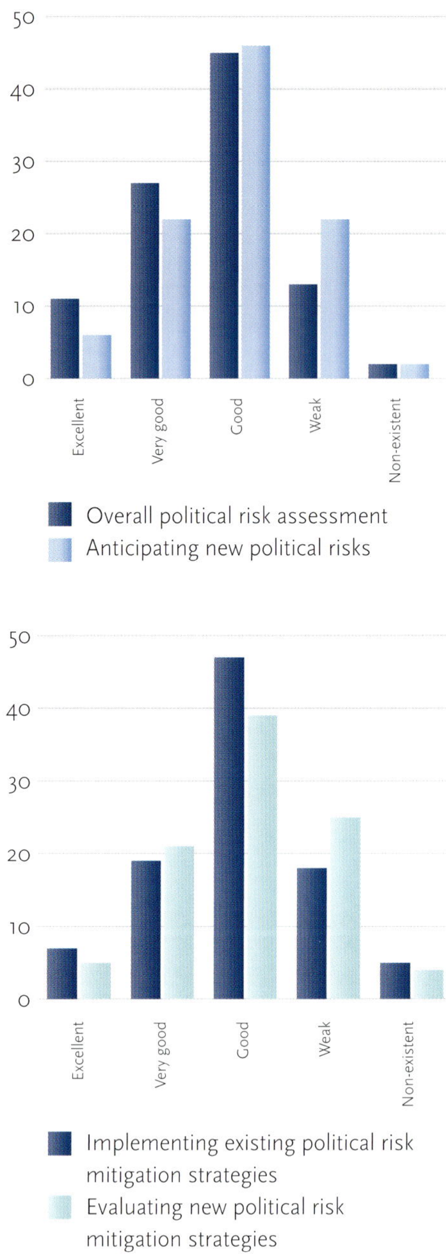

How would you rate your company's capabilities in the following areas?

Source: MIGA-EIU Political Risk Survey 2009.

Figure 2.4 Tools used to mitigate political risk in emerging markets

Percent of respondents

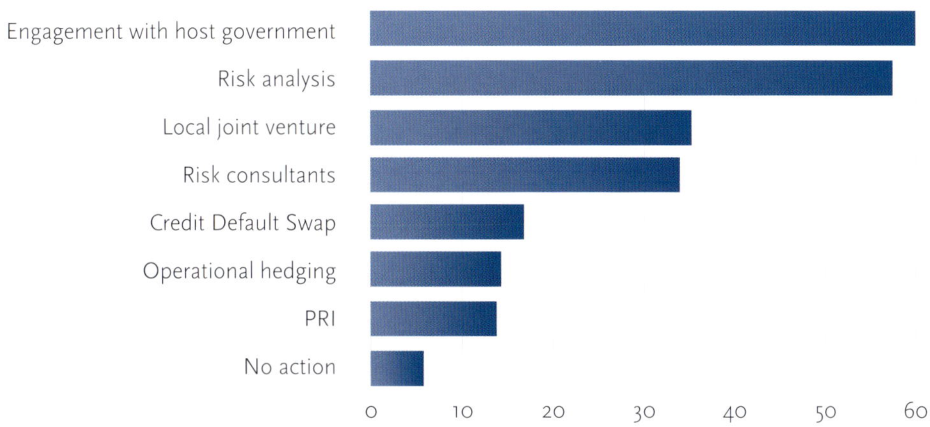

Which of the following does your company use as a tool for political risk mitigation? Select all that apply.

Source: MIGA-EIU Political Risk Survey 2009.
Note: Percentages add up to more than 100 percent due to multiple selections.

Table 2.1. Tools for mitigating political risk in emerging markets by sector

Percent of respondents

Sector	Local engagement	Risk analysis	Local joint venture	Risk consultants	CDS*	Operational hedging	PRI
Financial	54	58	31	33	32	14	21
Manufacturing	64	59	33	38	17	16	11
Services	63	54	33	29	11	17	13
Utilities and communications	55	59	48	35	8	6	14
Primary	57	61	48	35	2	12	6

* *Credit default swap.*
Source: MIGA-EIU Political Risk Survey 2009.
Note: Percentages add up to more than 100 percent due to multiple selections.

Figure 2.5 PRI usage by perceived riskiness of investment destination

Percent of respondents

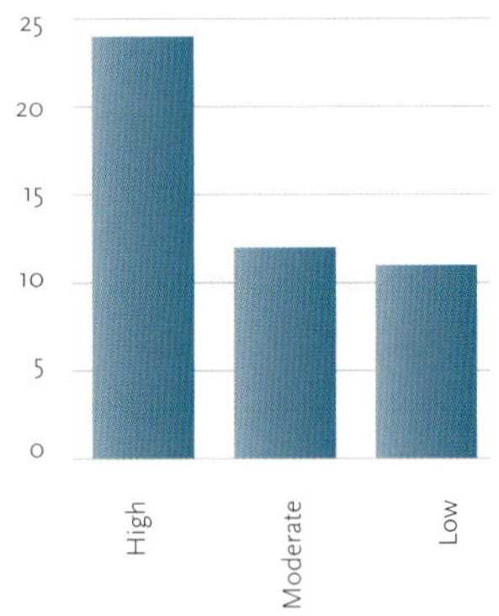

Proportion of respondents that use political risk insurance segmented by the perceived riskiness of their investment destinations.

Source: MIGA-EIU Political Risk Survey 2009.

Figure 2.6 PRI usage by ability to implement existing political risk mitigation strategy

Percent of respondents

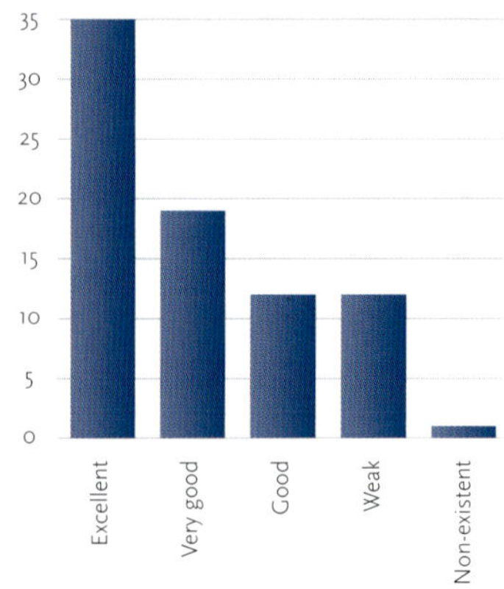

Proportion of respondents using PRI segmented by their ability to implement existing political risk mitigation strategies.

Source: MIGA-EIU Political Risk Survey 2009.

insurance is a specialized product reserved for investment environments they perceived to be the riskiest (figure 2.5).

The views of investors also confirmed that there is a link between respondents' ability to implement risk mitigation strategies and their decision to contract political risk insurance (figure 2.6). Investors best able to implement existing risk mitigation strategies reportedly used political risk insurance three times more frequently than investors with limited ability. Accordingly, only 1 percent of investors who reported having "non-existent" ability to implement risk mitigation strategies used political risk insurance. Furthermore, investors' ability to implement existing risk management strategies did not appear to be related to the level of risk of the investment destinations.[26] The latter finding lends support to the importance of creating awareness of political risk and risk mitigation mechanisms among investors.

Limited overall usage of political risk insurance as a risk mitigation tool at present, however, does not imply a lack of interest. When asked if they expected their company to consider political risk insurance for their investments abroad in the future, 40 percent of investors answered in the affirmative.[27] Among investors who rated their political risk assessment capabilities as excellent, the proportion was even higher: 54 percent expected their company to consider political risk insurance going forward.

Investors from Emerging Markets: Political Risk Perceptions and Mitigation

Growing flows of FDI from emerging markets (chapter 1) raise questions about perceptions of political risks by MNEs headquartered in these countries, and about how these perceptions shape their investment decisions. The survey of companies from Brazil, the Russian Federation, India and China conducted for this report highlights that concerns over political risks parallel their bullish investment intentions: political risk ranked first among concerns when investing in developing countries, both this year and over the next three years (figure 2.7). The financial crisis itself, however, did not alter the political risk perceptions of 61 percent of respondents when it comes to their main investment destinations; but another 27 percent of respondents perceived political risk to have worsened.

Box 2.2 Selected factors impacting investor demand for political risk insurance

A study conducted in 2007 for MIGA by PricewaterhouseCoopers found that the use of PRI by investors depended on a number of factors:

Country conditions and ratings
Evidence of heightened political risks (e.g. protectionism, resource nationalization, suspension of global trade agreements, change in country ratings) in the host country increases the demand for PRI.

Internal guidelines
Corporate guidelines and internal standards may require the purchase of PRI for certain projects and country destinations.

Investor/lender risk appetite
The project's sector and investment horizon, as well as knowledge and previous experience in the destination country, influence the risk appetite of investors and lenders and their demand for PRI. More extensive knowledge, however, may either lead to a more informed PRI purchase or placement through other means (e.g. self-insurance).

Dispute resolution mechanism
Investors' comfort level with the destination country's dispute resolution mechanism affects the demand for PRI. Some form of dispute resolution should be in place for PRI to be contracted.

Unavailability of comprehensive insurance
Investors prefer to bundle insurance coverage if possible, and lack of this alternative can lead to the purchase of PRI as a stand-alone product.

Cost of PRI
Investor demand for PRI is affected by premiums.

Availability of discretionary insurance following traditional insurance programs already in place
Investors may increase existing PRI coverage in soft pricing markets, and reduce PRI coverage in hard pricing markets.

Prior PRI claims experience
Any prior claims experience (favorable or unfavorable) can impact the decision to purchase PRI. Evidence of claim payments and process transparency favorably influence demand for PRI.

Competitiveness of debt markets
As competition to fund various projects increases, some lenders' requirement for investors to acquire PRI may diminish.

Source: PricewaterhouseCoopers, 2007.

Political risk was the leading concern this year for Russian and Brazilian investors, as well as for Indian investors (jointly with macroeconomic instability) and the second most significant concern for Chinese investors. Except for the Russian Federation, political risk remained the foremost concern over the medium term, as the expected recovery of the world economy diminished the relative importance of concerns related to the crisis and recession. The prominence of economic concerns for Russian investors may suggest that they anticipate the effects of the financial crisis to linger on.

While investors from emerging markets view political risk as a significant constraint on investment plans, they differ over the type of political risk that is of greatest concern. Overall, most investors from the BRICs considered breach of contract as the principal political risk this year and over the next three years (on par with transfer and convertibility restrictions for the latter). This was followed closely by transfer and convertibility restrictions and non-honoring of sovereign guarantees. The aggregate findings, however, mask important differences among the four countries regarding what each considers being the most worrisome political risk (figure 2.8). Political violence offers the sharpest contrast in relative weight of political risks for BRICs investors: it was considered the most significant risk for Chinese investors over the next three years, but it was of least concern for investors from Brazil and the Russian Federation.

Yet MNEs from the BRICs invest in developing countries they consider risky. Investors from Brazil, the Russian

Figure 2.7 Main foreign investment constraints for investors from the BRICs

Percent of respondents

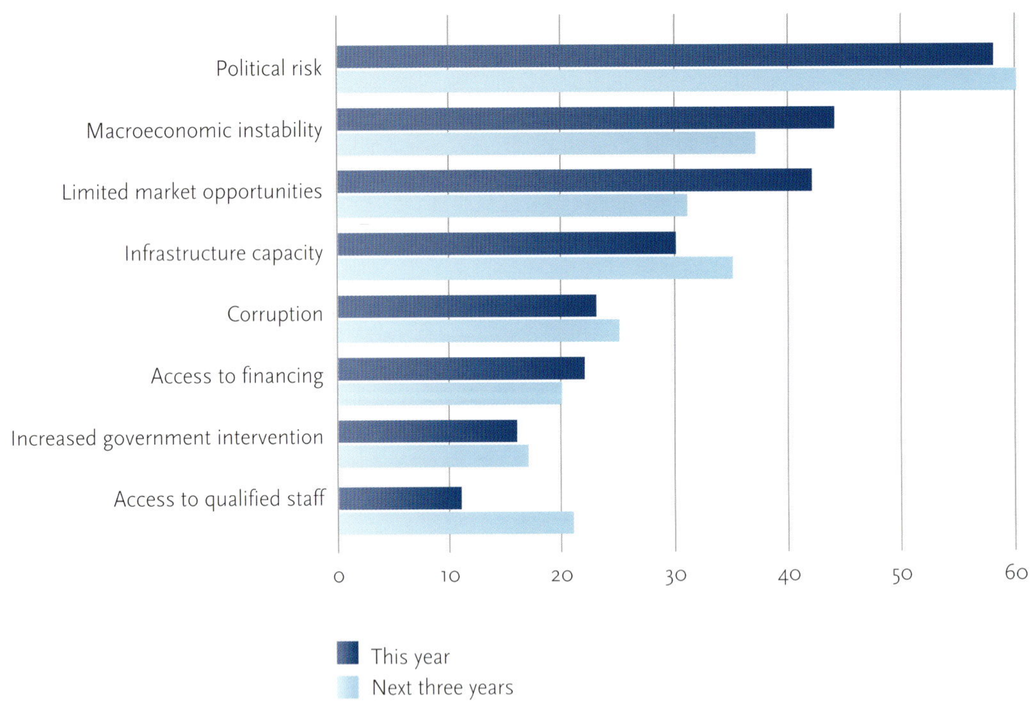

In your opinion, which of the following factors will pose the greatest constraint on investment by your company in emerging markets this year and over the next three years?

Source: MIGA-VCC Political Risk Survey in the BRICs 2009.
Note: Percentages add up to more than 100 percent due to multiple selections.

Figure 2.8 Top political risks for investors from the BRICs

Percent of respondents

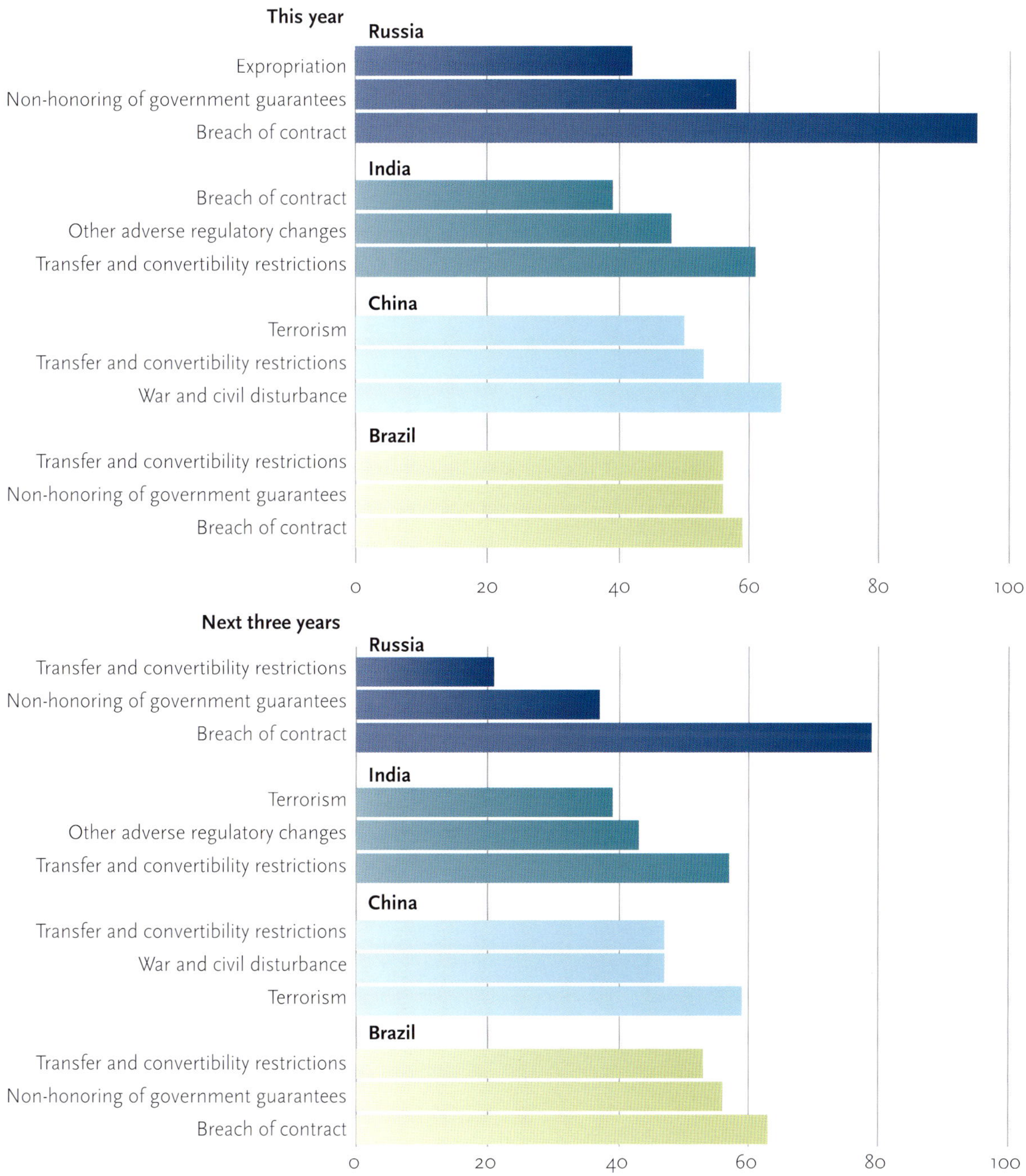

In your opinion, which types of political risk are of most concern to your company when investing in emerging markets?

Source: MIGA-VCC Political Risk Survey in the BRICs 2009.
Note: Top three responses. Percentages add up to more than 100 percent due to multiple selections.

Federation, India and China all cited as a top investment destination this year and over the next thee year at least one country that also appeared in the list of their perceived riskiest countries. Argentina and Venezuela (R.B. de), for example, were among the largest five recipients of Brazilian FDI this year, and were also perceived by Brazilian investors as having very high or high political risk. Likewise Russian MNEs perceived their largest investment destinations (the members of the Commonwealth of Independent States) as highly risky. Some respondents argued that business strategy and profitable opportunities took precedence over political risk—except in cases of political violence—in determining where to invest.

Yet 11 percent of BRIC respondents said they did not mitigate political risks at all—compared to 6 percent in the global survey. The principal reason given by investors from the BRICs for not mitigating political risks was the lack of appropriate tools and products. This was the main objection for investors from Brazil, China and the Russian Federation and the second most important for Indian companies (figure 2.9). Over a third of BRIC respondents also felt that the level of risk in their destination countries did not warrant mitigating political risk. A substantial minority (28 percent) said they were unaware of specific products and tools available; about a third of Indian MNEs cited their lack of knowledge in that area, despite the long existence of ECGC, the country's public provider of investment insurance.

Figure 2.9 Reasons cited for not mitigating political risks by MNEs from the BRICs
Percent of respondents

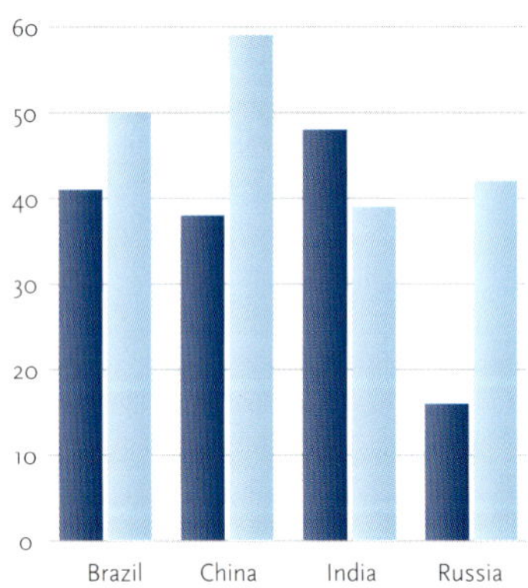

What are the primary reasons your company does not use tools or products to mitigate political risks?

Source: MIGA-VCC Political Risk Survey in the BRICs 2009.
Note: Top two responses. Percentages add up to more than 100 percent due to multiple selections.

To the extent that they do mitigate political risk, MNEs from the BRICs use primarily informal and internal means to do so; they do not differ from respondents in the global survey on that account. Some respondents mentioned that an additional benefit of such indirect or informal risk mitigation techniques was their low cost, compared to more formal instruments. The most popular tools are producing political risk analysis and assessments, engaging with host country governments and engaging in joint ventures and alliances with host country firms (figure 2.10). Most MNEs from the Russian Federation, for example, viewed engaging with host country governments as the most effective means of shielding themselves against political risk. Political risk analysis and concluding joint ventures with local firms—the favorite choices of Chinese, Indian and Brazilian respondents—were also ranked as the preferred mitigation method by investors from the countries in the global survey.

The financial crisis enhanced the attractiveness of risk mitigation tools for one in three BRICs respondents (mostly Chinese companies).

At present, PRI ranks low amongst risk mitigation tools used by BRICs investors. This may suggest that much needs to be done by the political risk insurance industry to reach out to these emerging investors (chapter 3). Russian MNEs are an exception, however, in that political risk insurance was the second most popular tool, after engagement with host country governments. The most common cover sought by the BRICs investors that used PRI was for breach of contract (mostly Russian companies), followed by transfer and convertibility restrictions, and expropriation.

Although political risk insurance ranked low as a current risk mitigation tool, more than half of BRICs respondents said they would consider PRI going forward (figure 2.11; see also chapter 3 on political risk insurance products available to MNEs from emerging markets). Chinese and Indian investors were the most enthusiastic. Russian companies—already significant users of political risk insurance—were more skeptical.

Amongst respondents using insurance, some MNEs from India mentioned they used PRI partly in response to requirements from banks financing their investments. Others from China and India mentioned that they used PRI because indirect or informal risk mitigation methods

FIGURE 2.10 POLITICAL RISK MITIGATION TOOLS USED BY MNEs FROM THE BRICs

Percent of respondents

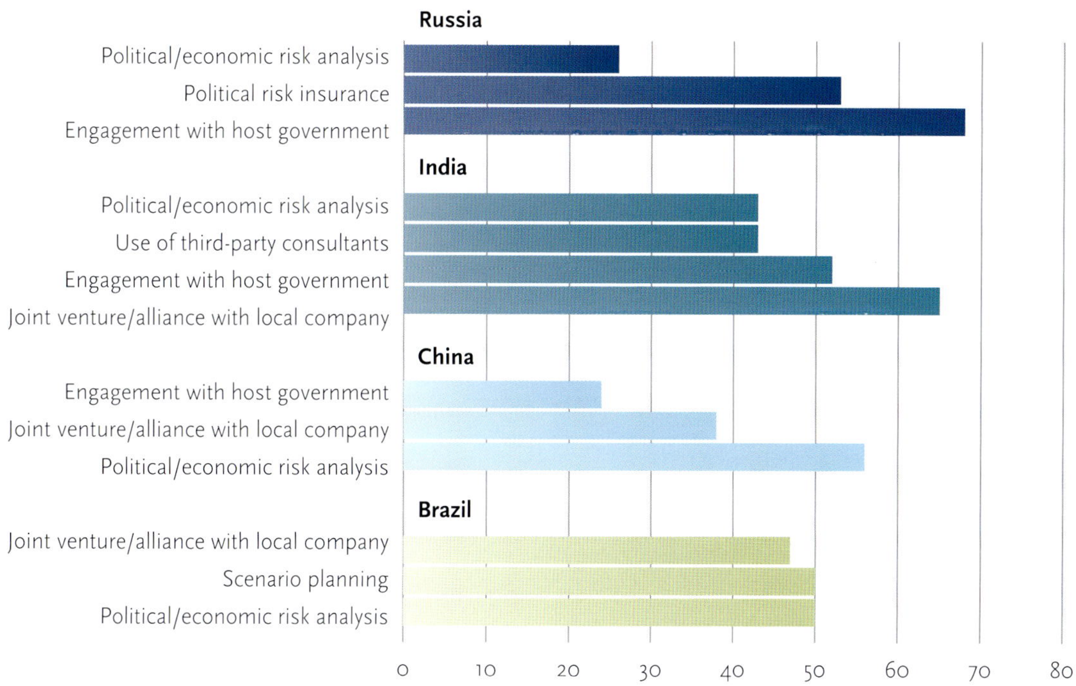

Which of the following does your company use as a tool for political risk mitigation?

Source: MIGA-VCC Political Risk Survey in the BRICs 2009.
Note: Top three responses. Percentages add up to more than 100 percent due to multiple selections.

were not appropriate for covering risks of war, civil disturbance or terrorism. Some respondents felt that political risk insurance provides more effective coverage against political violence—although this was not reflected in the types of political risk coverage most frequently purchased.

Some respondents, on the other hand, felt that PRI defines political risks too narrowly, which reduces their appeal. Supply chain disruptions were cited as an example of loss that respondents thought as not covered by the formal mitigation products. Cost, cumbersome contracting process and confusing offering were also cited as factors inhibiting mitigation through insurance. Some respondents argued that the size of their investments was too small to justify contracting PRI.

When asked to self-evaluate their risk assessment capabilities, investors from the BRICs thought well of their own abilities to assess political risk, but they were much less confident in their abilities to anticipate new risks. Most respondents viewed their abilities to implement risk mitigation strategies as good (the midpoint between their five options), but felt less able to implement new mitigation strategies. Chinese MNEs felt particularly ill equipped to evaluate risk mitigation strategies, and Indian MNEs felt weak in their ability to assign roles and responsibilities for political risk management.

The findings of the BRIC survey mirror sentiments of executives from other major emerging-market FDI sources, such as Singapore (box 2.6).

Box 2.3 Political risk perceptions of Singaporean enterprises

With FDI outflows averaging $16 billion annually during 2005-2008, Singapore is an important hub for regional and international investment. Asia is the top destination of Singapore's FDI, with 46 percent of its outward stock located there (as of 2007): China, Malaysia, Indonesia, Hong Kong SAR, China and Thailand are major destinations. More than half of its outward investment is concentrated in financial services and just over a fifth is in manufacturing.

Singapore has weathered the financial crisis well, with investors becoming more optimistic about opportunities in the region. International Enterprises Singapore, an agency of the Ministry of Trade and Industry, collaborated with MIGA in July and August 2009 to gather perspectives from executives of Singapore-headquartered companies on investment and political risk. Singaporean companies were well placed to discuss issues relating to overseas expansion as some two thirds of them are planning to increase investment this year and nearly all plan to expand abroad in the aftermath of the crisis.

At the same time Singaporean companies are becoming more aware of political risk. Executives, mostly from enterprises in the manufacturing and services sectors, expressed political risk to be one of their top two constraints on investment this year and their top concern going forward. And although for the majority of these executives the financial crisis did not change their perceptions of political risks in their target markets, nor did it affect their interest in managing these risks, almost two thirds expected their companies to consider political risk insurance going forward.

Approximately half of the Singaporean executives assessed their own capacity for implementing, evaluating and managing risk mitigations strategies as weak or non-existent. However, they considered their ability to evaluate risks to be better, and identified the most pressing political risks facing their operations to be transfer and convertibility, breach of contract and regulatory changes, both now and going forward. The risk of expropriation was the fastest growing concern.

Source: International Enterprises Singapore, and Singapore Department of Statistics, 2009

Figure 2.11 Interest in PRI from BRICs investors

Percent of respondents

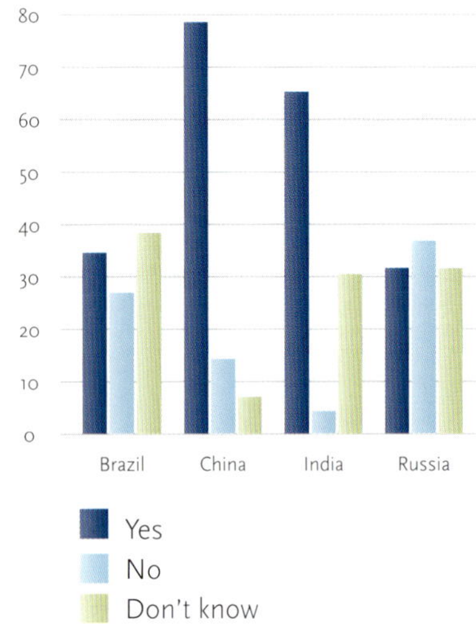

Moving forward, do you expect your company to consider political risk insurance for its investments abroad?

Source: MIGA-VCC Political Risk Survey in the BRICs 2009.

* * *

The BRIC and global surveys suggest that the attitude of investors from emerging markets toward political risk may overall not be very different than those from industrialized countries. Respondents from both surveys ranked political risk as a top concern when investing in developing countries in the short and medium term—which challenges the view that investors from emerging markets are comfortable with political perils.

That the salience of political risk relative to other concerns does not translate into high usage of political risk insurance suggests that investors are confident they can manage most risks effectively without resorting to formal mitigation products. Indeed, they use a wide range of methods to do so. This could reflect confidence in the stability of the handful of investment destinations that absorb most FDI to developing countries, or sufficient familiarity with these destinations and the risks involved. PRI is more often used for destinations considered the riskiest, although a number of other factors also influence whether investors turn to insurance.

Yet, the surveys also highlight the need for the PRI industry to further reach out to investors, in particular those from emerging markets.

Chapter Two —Endnotes

1 *This report covers political perils in developing countries only, and focuses on FDI. The impact of political risk on other forms of private capital flows is beyond the scope of this report.*

2 *Luo (2008).*

3 *For a discussion of the history of the relationship between host country governments and multinational enterprises, see Vernon (1971).*

4 *Minor (1994).*

5 *Wiener (1996).*

6 *UNCTAD (2006), table I.11.*

7 *The World Bank's Doing Business 2010 recorded 287 such reforms in 131 economies between June 2008 and May. 2009, 20 percent more than in the year before.*

8 *Between 1991 and 2000, approximately 1,600 BITs were signed, compared to 386 signed in the 1980s and 166 in the 1970s. By end 2008, over 2,600 BITs were in place. Data provided by UNCTAD (2009a).*

9 *By end 2008, over 270 free trade agreements with extensive investment provisions existed. UNCTAD (2009a).*

10 *World Bank (2009), UNCTAD (2009).*

11 *Sauvant (2009).*

12 *See "Addressing Political Risk in the Extractive Sector", internet feature at (http://www.pri-center.com/feature/index.cfm?fid=13).*

13 *For a discussion of political risk in the energy sector, see Sachs (2007).*

14 *Control Risks (2007) and Lloyd's and Control Risks (2009).*

15 *Around 35 percent of respondents highlighted war and civil disturbance as major area of concern, while close to 25 percent of them mentioned terrorism. In aggregate, the proportion of respondents concerned about political violence is 43 percent.*

16 *From the underlying indicators rated in EIU's Risk Briefing, an aggregate measure of political risk was constructed that corresponded closely to the definition of political risk used for this report. It was based on the ratings of the risk of armed conflict, terrorism, violent demonstrations, social unrest, various measures of governmental instability, external tensions, enforceability of contracts, expropriation, and the risk of the imposition of current and capital account controls.*

17 *Remittance flows to developing countries are projected by the World Bank to decline by 6.1 percent in 2009 from $338 billion in 2008. See Ratha et al. (2009).*

18 *World Bank (2009)*

19 *Lloyd's and Control Risks (2009), Eurasia Group (2009).*

20 *World Bank (2009).*

21 *World Bank (2009), table 3.2.*

22 *For a full list of the countries that have received assistance to address short-term balance of payments problems from the IMF, see IMF (2009).*

23 *World Bank (2009).*

24 *For a discussion and a list of government policies that might discriminate against FDI and trade, see Thomsen (2009).*

25 *OECD (2009), UNCTAD (2009b), and OECD, UNCTAD, and WTO (2009).*

26 *Respondents with self-reported "excellent" and "non-existent" ability to implement existing risk mitigation strategies invest in countries with a similar risk profile. The level of risk in investment destinations of respondents with "excellent" abilities averages 2.14 (on a scale of 1 to 3, where 1 is low and 3 is high) and 2.19 for respondents with non-existent abilities. As compared to this, investment destinations of respondents with "good" abilities averaged 2.11 in the same scale.*

27 *Respondents from the primary sector were the least likely to consider political risk insurance in the future: only 31 percent said they would, compared to 37 percent in manufacturing, 40 percent in utilities, transport, storage and communications, 44 percent in services and 44 percent in the financial sector.*

CHAPTER THREE

THE POLITICAL RISK INSURANCE INDUSTRY: *A VIEW FROM THE SUPPLY SIDE*

Overview

Robust appetite for investment in emerging markets in the medium term and the rising prominence of South-based investors present both challenges and opportunities for the investment insurance side of the PRI industry. This changing global environment, combined with a greater awareness of political risks on the part of investors, places the industry in a position to expand its reach and help promote the expected rebound of FDI to emerging markets. Over the past two decades, only a small percentage of FDI to emerging economies has been insured. However, PRI—although not a key determinant of FDI flows—can play an important role in restoring investor confidence and in facilitating investments of high development impact (such as in infrastructure and extractive industries) and investments into underserved markets (such as poorer countries and conflict-affected environments).

Today, the PRI industry is well positioned to support the recovery of FDI to emerging economies. It has grown from a minimal presence twenty years ago to a well-established market today, with a size, in terms of premiums for investment insurance, in the order of $1 billion.[1] The industry is now mature and resilient, having been shaped by numerous shocks in the past two decades. Over the years, its underwriting standards and processes have strengthened, and its exposure has become more diversified and spread over a large number of well capitalized and informed carriers, both in the private and public segments of the market. These developments position the industry well for a post-crisis global investment landscape where resource nationalism, political upheavals and currency instability in certain emerging markets may continue to drive the demand for PRI.

In some segments of the private market, the crisis has led to higher selectivity and stricter underwriting conditions, and capacity has been reduced for several countries. However, the public insurers—the export credit agencies (ECAs) and multilaterals—are well placed to fill any potential gaps because they do not face the same capacity constraints as their private counterparts (see box 3.5 on the differences between public and private insurers). This highlights the role of the public insurers in providing stability and maintaining capacity in the PRI market during uncertain times. At present, several ECAs are being encouraged by their governments to support their national investors and play an enhanced role in both trade credit and investment insurance to support the global economic recovery. Going forward, continued cooperation between the public and private segments of the PRI market will become increasingly important, suggesting a strong role for the Berne Union (BU), as the leading association of investment insurers and export credit agencies, in bringing these groups together (see box 3.1 on the activities of the BU).

The changing dynamics of world investment, with the rising power of South-based investors and their concerns over political risks, presents both opportunities and challenges for the PRI market. The industry is already reaching out to this fast-growing investor base. Some of the South-based national public insurers that had traditionally focused on export cover are expanding their PRI for investment, while the private market is extending its global reach in places such as Singapore, which is developing into a regional insurance hub. But the industry still needs to promote its services and improve investor awareness of the PRI product in emerging economies. It also needs to continue adapting its product offerings to meet the evolving demands of investors in a post-crisis investment landscape.

Political Risk Insurance and FDI

The rise of FDI to emerging markets over the past decade has encouraged the expansion of the PRI industry, which has grown particularly rapidly since 2003 (figure 3.1).[2] The growth of PRI is not just related to levels of new foreign investment in emerging markets but to a host of other factors as well that affect both investors' decisions to use PRI (chapter 2, box 2.2) and the insurance industry's ability to provide the needed coverage.

Historically, investors have sought increased levels of PRI for certain countries and sectors following global crises and high profile claims that have shaken confidence and heightened awareness of political risks. In the early 1980s, PRI for emerging market investments increased in part due to concerns arising from the financial crisis at the time and from the wave of expropriations in the late 1970s, such as those linked to the rise of the Sandanistas in Nicaragua and the fall of the Shah of Iran. PRI covered around 20-25 percent of emerging market FDI then, as shown in figure 3.2, which covers PRI provided by BU members only.[3]

Since the late 1980s, FDI has been on an upward trend while the portion of FDI covered by PRI has been on a downward trend, suggesting a growing confidence in emerging economies as investment destinations. The decade of the 1990s saw a steady increase in FDI to these markets as a result of globalization, liberalization and the opportunities created for foreign investment by the wave of privatizations, but the proportion of FDI covered by PRI was considerably smaller than in the early 1980s. In the latter half of the 1990s, project financing from banks grew to support investments in infrastructure, fuelling the demand for PRI. Although this encouraged the growth of the private insurance market, the proportion of FDI covered by PRI from BU members (largely ECAs at the time) was on a downward trend (boxes 3.3 and 3.6).

The rapid growth of FDI to emerging markets between 2003 and 2008 generated further demand for PRI (figure 3.1). However, although PRI provided by BU members increased in absolute terms (and this included a significant portion of private insurers who had become members by that time), the ratio of PRI to FDI remained low at around 10 percent. The decline in the PRI/FDI ratio reflected the extent to which the overall investment environment in emerging economies was viewed as benign, even though there was some country differentiation based on concerns about resource nationalism (particularly in parts of Latin America and Africa) and political violence in certain parts of the world.

Figure 3.1 FDI flows and New PRI of Berne Union Members
$ billion

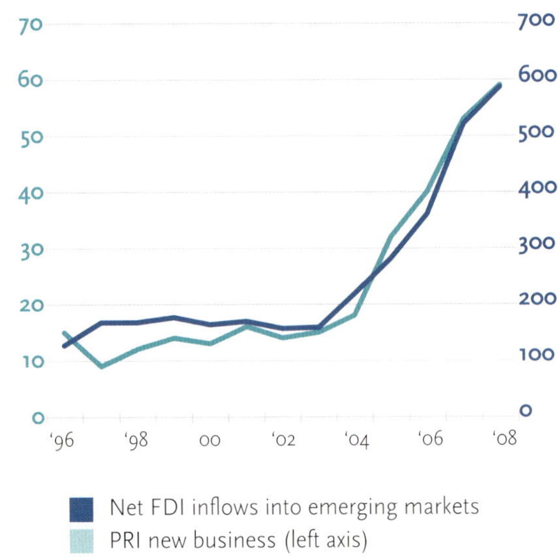

Source: World Bank 2009 and Berne Union 2009.

Although FDI to emerging markets declined significantly in 2009 (chapter 1), it is still expected to be high compared to historic levels and to rebound in 2010. This continued interest in investing in emerging markets, combined with a changing awareness of risk as the global economic downturn weighs on investors' minds, suggests that PRI in relation to FDI could potentially rise. A significant minority of investors surveyed for this report (chapter 2) expressed an interest in risk mitigation tools as a result of the crisis. Whether this potential demand translates into more insurance coverage going forward depends on how both governments and the PRI industry respond in a post-crisis environment.

Box 3.1 The Berne Union

The Berne Union (BU) was founded in 1934 in order to promote international acceptance of sound principles in export credit and investment insurance and to exchange information relating to these activities. Today, the BU has 73 members (including Prague Club members) comprising mainly export credit agencies (ECAs), multilaterals and private insurers (see annex 6).[4] Most ECAs and multilaterals are BU members, as are large private insurers such as AIG (now Chartis Insurance), which joined in 1999, followed by Zurich, Sovereign Risk Insurance Ltd. and then Chubb in 2004. In October 2008, Hiscox became the first private insurer underwriting in Lloyd's to join the BU. The BU plays an important role in bringing together the public and private insurers to enhance cooperation and information sharing. Members meet on a regular basis to discuss industry trends and challenges. In recent years, there has been a concerted effort on the part of the BU Secretariat to promote transparency and disclosure in the industry and to represent member interests in order to promote global trade and investment.

Box 3.2 Political Risk Insurance and its Benefits

PRI captures most, but not all, non-commercial risks. It covers political events, including the direct and indirect actions of host governments, which negatively impact investments and are not promptly or adequately compensated for. PRI refers to a broad range of product lines that include both trade credit and investment insurance. For the purposes of this report, it is applied exclusively to investment insurance.

In addition to providing compensatory value in the event of claims, PRI can help investors access finance and often on better terms, increasing the tenors and size of available loans. Investors are often required to get this insurance in order to obtain financing from banks. For lenders, PRI can provide regulatory relief from country risk provisioning requirements. PRI can also help deter harmful actions by host governments, help resolve investment disputes and provide access to best practices in environmental and social standards.

The following are the political risks commonly insured by the PRI industry. It is important to note however, that there are differences in the terminology and definitions used by the various insurers, particularly between the public and private insurers.

Expropriation: PRI protects against losses due to host government actions that may reduce or eliminate ownership or control. It covers outright confiscations, expropriations and nationalizations, as well as losses resulting from a series of acts that over time have an expropriatory effect.

Currency Inconvertibility and Transfer Restrictions: PRI protects against losses arising from an investor's inability to convert local currency into foreign exchange and transfer it out of the host country. It also covers excessive delays in acquiring foreign exchange. Typically, this coverage applies to the interruption of interest payments or repatriation of capital or dividends due to currency restrictions. It does not cover devaluation risk..

Political Violence: (War, Terrorism and Civil Disturbance): PRI protects against losses due to the damage of tangible assets or business interruption caused by war, insurrection, rebellion, revolution, civil war, vandalism, sabotage, civil disturbance, strikes, riots and terrorism. Coverage usually applies to politically motivated acts. Certain insurers offer terrorism coverage on a stand-alone basis to supplement property insurance policies, which have largely excluded terrorism as a peril since September 11.

Breach of Contract/Arbitration Award Default: PRI protects against losses arising from a host government's breach or repudiation of a contractual agreement with an investor. Claims are usually payable only after an investor has invoked a dispute resolution mechanism (such as arbitration), obtained an award for damages and the host government has failed to honor the award.

Non-Honoring of Sovereign Financial Obligations: PRI protects against losses resulting from a government's failure to make a payment when due under an unconditional financial payment obligation or guarantee given in favor of a project that otherwise meets an insurer's requirements. It does not require the investor to obtain an arbitral award. This coverage is usually applicable in situations when a sovereign's financial payment obligation is unconditional and not subject to defenses.

Figure 3.2 Ratio of PRI to FDI for Emerging Markets
Percent

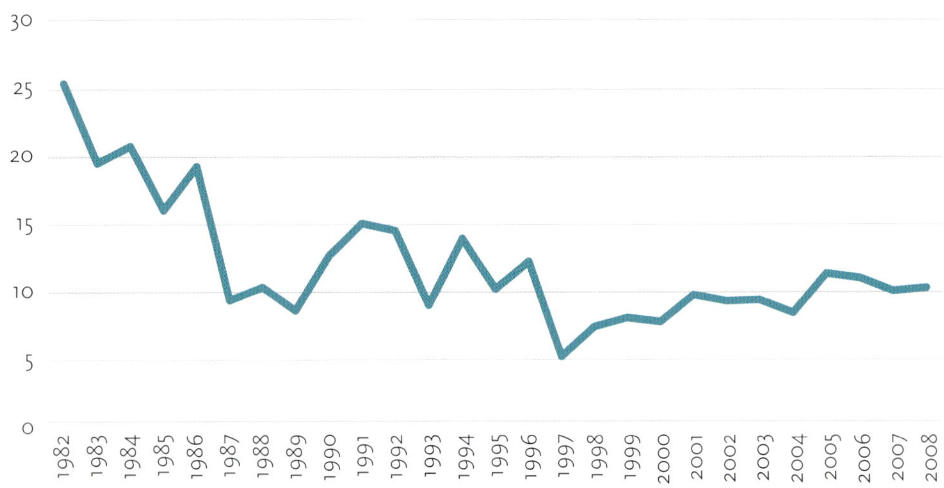

Source: World Bank 2009 and Berne Union 2009.
Note: Figures relate to new PRI from Berne Union members only and to net FDI inflows each year.

Trends in the PRI Industry

The PRI industry is well positioned to respond to any potential growth in demand for insurance when the post-crisis recovery takes off. It is now mature and resilient having grown significantly since its modest origins around the time of the Second World War. Today, the market is well diversified with a broad range of products. It has been shaped by numerous crises and events over the past decade, which have informed better practices within the industry, refined the product offerings, improved monitoring and indemnity standards, and strengthened underwriting procedures (see box 3.6 on the evolution of the PRI industry).

In the late 1990s, the surge in privatization activities in emerging economies, particularly in infrastructure, encouraged the growth and diversification of the private market—new entrants stimulated competition and started offering long tenors to cover large, complex projects. This increased the market share of private providers and gave rise to improved cooperation between public and private insurers through reinsurance and coinsurance arrangements. Such collaborations increased capacity in the marketplace. The Asian and Russian financial crises of the late 1990s, as well as an increase in investor disputes and claims caused by the failure of governments to honor their contractual obligations, highlighted product weaknesses and eventually put pressure on insurers to refine product offerings and provide new coverages to meet investor needs.

A few years later, September 11 and the Argentine crisis demonstrated the extreme loss potential for the industry resulting from terrorism and a country's economic meltdown. The events of September 11 transformed terrorism insurance into a catastrophe product and made the availability of reinsurance a key determinant of private market capacity. The Argentine crisis raised questions about the value of PRI, but also demonstrated that the industry paid claims, and highlighted the ability of the BU to represent its members' interests (box 3.4).

The PRI industry's historical development, as well as its experience with claims, has helped make it more resilient over time. It has been able to build reserves in good years to meet potential claims in tougher times. Historically, there have been very few claims each year and they have represented a small portion of the maximum limit of liability of BU members. Between 1996 and 2008,

BU members paid total claims of around $795 million.[5] Recoveries of claims for BU members over this period averaged around 45 percent. Lloyd's syndicates are reported to have paid about $608 million in expropriation claims during the same period.

In addition to being resilient, the PRI industry has adapted its products over the past decade to respond to investor demands. The private market has been through a significant phase of product refinement with regard to political violence policies, particularly since September 11. These policies now encompass, in combination, all political perils spanning terrorism through to riot and civil disturbance, insurrection to rebellion, and war on land to civil war. More recently, insurers have responded to pressure from investors to cover more than just arbitral awards (required under breach of contract cover). Today, many insurers provide non-honoring or non-payment cover for sovereign guarantors and borrowers without requiring investors to go through arbitration. Insurance policies are also becoming increasingly focused on identifying and defining investors' rights as the legal framework for FDI changes with improved bilateral and multilateral investment treaties. In spite of these innovations however, the PRI product has not always been fully understood nor has met investor expectations in the event of actual claims (as during the Argentine crisis discussed in box 3.4) This suggests a continuing need for product evolution and refinement.

The public and private segments of the PRI market have played complementary roles over time, although there have been some concerns about competition and crowding out. While the private PRI market is susceptible to sharp reductions in capacity, the public insurers are generally not constrained by this, so they can play an important role in stabilizing the market during uncertain times (box 3.5). The early 2000s highlighted the "cyclicality" of private PRI availability and the role of public insurers. It showed the contrast in the appetite for business in the late 1990s (when profits were high and attracted the capital needed to create capacity) with the post-September 11 period when initially the major losses eroded capital and decreased capacity in the Lloyd's segment of the private market, before reversing track again some years later (figure 3.4). Throughout this period, the public insurers, who are largely insulated from the broader property-casualty market cycles, helped dampen the amplitude of the cycles in the private market by maintaining adequate capacity, stable prices and tenors.

Today, ECAs and multilaterals can play an important role in augmenting the capacity of the private market to support the resurgence in FDI flows to emerging economies. They can potentially fill any gaps caused by reduced capacity for certain countries in the private market and can provide capacity for large projects through

Box 3.3 Overview of the PRI market

The PRI market includes three broad categories of providers and covers both export or trade credit and investment insurance. For the purposes of this report, PRI refers to investment insurance. The public PRI market comprises both national and multilateral PRI providers. The private market's PRI falls into two main categories: (i) political risk activities similar to those of the public insurers, such as coverage for investments in emerging markets against expropriation, political violence and other such risks; and (ii) emerging market non-payment insurance covering contract frustration and default by governments.

The National PRI Providers: They comprise national ECAs, export-import banks, export credit guarantee agencies and investment insurance entities, which focus on cross-border trade and investment, generally for constituents in their own countries. Euler Hermes—PwC (Germany), NEXI (Japan), OeKB (Austria) and Sinosure (China) account for about 38 percent of the market share of BU members.

The Multilaterals: The multilateral PRI providers include the African Trade Insurance Agency, the Inter-Arab Investment Guarantee Corporation, the Islamic Corporation for the Insurance of Investment and Export Credit, and the Multilateral Investment Guarantee Agency. Other multilateral agencies such as the World Bank, the Asian Development Bank, and the Inter-American Development Bank also provide risk mitigation instruments, such as partial risk guarantees.[6]

The Private PRI Market: The private underwriting market includes about 18 Lloyd's syndicates and about 10 private insurance companies. The majority of private insurers are based in three insurance centers—London, Bermuda and the United States (primarily New York)—and several of the larger insurers have offices in Singapore. The private PRI market forms part of a wider insurance market that offers protection from political perils either as "stand-alone" cover, or in combination with commercial credit risk cover. Due to the complex nature of the private market, brokers play an important role in promoting and sourcing PRI. Chartis Insurance (USA), Zurich (USA), Sovereign Risk Insurance Ltd. (Bermuda) and Chubb (USA) account for about 43 percent of the market share of BU members.

The Reinsurers: Reinsurance companies write PRI-related coverage for both trade and investment. Reinsurance is an underlying factor driving both pricing and capacity in the private market. Some of the top reinsurers include Munich Re and Hannover Re of Germany, Swiss Re of Switzerland, and Berkshire Hathaway/General Re of the USA. ECAs and multilaterals also participate as reinsurers of PRI, although on a smaller scale.

Source: Data on national and private providers from the Berne Union.

Box 3.4 Lessons from the Argentine Crisis

In the 1990s, Argentina was amongst the top recipients of FDI to emerging markets. Although the amount of total new FDI covered by PRI during the decade was low (figure 3.2), many PRI providers were close to reaching their maximum capacity for Argentina. By end 1999, however, the Asian and Russian crises had exposed the weaknesses of the Argentine economy, particularly the one-to-one peso to dollar peg that had been introduced in 1992. In the following years, after failing to engineer a recession-induced price realignment that would keep the peg in place, the economy deteriorated to such an extent that political and social pressures led to the fall of the government, followed by a period of political instability. Between November 2001 and January 2002, the government froze all bank deposits and passed an "Emergency Law" that allowed it to implement a series of measures to prevent foreign capital outflows. This law revoked the dollar peg and established a new, lower exchange rate. It converted all domestic loans denominated in foreign currency into local currency at the post-devaluation exchange rate, and froze bank deposits after converting them to pesos at the pre-devaluation parity (which became known as "pesification", whose asymmetric treatment of banks' balance sheets meant that the financial sector essentially became insolvent overnight). The law also required prior approvals for transfer of foreign currency for any purpose, including servicing foreign loans. In addition, the law declared that all public contracts that included adjustment and indexation clauses based on foreign currency were no longer in effect, but required tariffs to be frozen at the pre-devaluation exchange rate.

Argentina's economic and political crisis became a test case for the PRI industry, as many insurers were faced with claims and disputes. For the first time, a country's economic meltdown had triggered disputes and potential claims under different covers, including breach of contract, expropriation, transfer restriction and civil disturbance. Delays on loan repayments, due to the freezing of bank deposits and the need to obtain government approval to service foreign loans, resulted in transfer restrictions claims, and the revocation of the Convertibility Law gave rise to expropriation claims as investors argued their investments were no longer viable. A high profile example was the case of Ponderosa Assets Pvt. Ltd, which triggered the payment of a claim by OPIC. Ponderosa had to write off its investment in Argentina after the tariffs it charged for gas distribution were frozen and set in pesos using an overvalued exchange rate. The company obtained an arbitral award from the International Centre for Settlement of Investment Disputes (ICSID), which ruled that the Argentine government had breached the "fair and equitable standard" contained in the BIT between Argentina and the United States.

The consequences of the Argentine crisis on the PRI industry were significant. For transfer and convertibility coverages, the industry was able to obtain an exception for all BU members from the Central Bank, thereby allowing borrowers whose foreign loans were insured by BU members to convert local currency into dollars. This enabled them to service their loans on time. At the same time, however, the market faced many claims from banks in Argentina that were not paid, because the borrowers lacked the necessary local currency to effect a valid inconvertibility claim. These losses were considered by many insurers to be commercial in nature and therefore not within the scope of most PRI policies. Many banks began to question the value of PRI in the aftermath of the Argentine crisis, which led to increasing demand for comprehensive cover.[7] Despite some disputes with insureds, claims were paid; it is estimated that about $124 million was paid out between 2002 and 2006.[8] Finally, and more importantly for expropriation and breach of contract coverages, the crisis tested the strength of BITs, which protect investor rights more broadly than traditional PRI contracts. Forty-eight treaty cases, involving either expropriation and/or breach of contract coverages, have been filed against Argentina since 2001—45 cases with ICSID and three under the United Nations Commission on International Trade Law (UNCITRAL) Rules. With 19 cases still pending, almost $1.2 billion has already been awarded against Argentina, including $508 million for claims that pre-date the emergency regulations. In cases where the arbitration has found in favor of the investor, however, the government has mostly failed to comply, leading to claims payments. It is also worth noting that in some cases, ICSID rejected submissions for expropriation (under the argument that the measures taken by authorities were not "expropriatory takings" but breaches of contractual obligations) that had been accepted by PRI providers, but awarded on the basis that the fair and equitable treatment provisions contained in BITs were breached. Since this discrepancy comes from the coverage language, as well as some of the case particularities, these examples are another reason why insureds have increased their demand for comprehensive coverage.

Sources: Berne Union 2009; Brown (2004).

coinsurance and reinsurance arrangements. They can also encourage investments into countries that are perceived to be high risk—where private insurers may not take exposure on their own—through such arrangements.

Impact of the Global Financial Crisis

The current global financial crisis has brought about a greater awareness of risk, and in mid-2009 certain segments of the PRI industry had taken a more conservative view of the new risk landscape. For example, Lloyd's mirrored the changing environment in a report issued in June 2009, which highlights some key points, namely that: (i) continuing economic turmoil could have a significant impact on the levels of instability and political risk for global businesses, and this may outlast the recession; (ii) investment climates in emerging markets may appear more investor-friendly in the short term, but expropriation risk may well rise in proportion to the severity of the recession; and (iii) investors and lenders must continue to assess expropriation risk on a country-by-country basis.[9]

Although losses for some private market participants in certain non-PRI lines of business have influenced the PRI industry's outlook, the market as a whole has functioned relatively well in the face of the global downturn.[10] BU members' investment insurance activities continued to expand in 2008; they booked $59 billion worth of new business, bringing their outstanding portfolio or maximum limit of liability in investment insurance to about $146 billion. However, almost all BU members saw new business decline in the first half of 2009 compared to 2008. Comparable figures are not available for the Lloyd's syndicates.

The PRI industry's size, risk diversification and robust underwriting standards and processes have helped ensure that the impact of the crisis has been absorbed by the market and that losses have been manageable so far. In some segments of the private market the crisis has led to higher selectivity and reduced capacity for certain countries. However, ECAs are playing a more active role in both trade credit and investment insurance to support the global economic recovery. The industry as a whole is therefore well positioned to respond to any increase in demand for PRI.

Claims. While there have been trade credit claims from all over the world since late 2008, investment insurance claims have so far been limited. Even the expropriation

Figure 3.3 Claims Paid, Recoveries and Premiums of BU Members
$ million

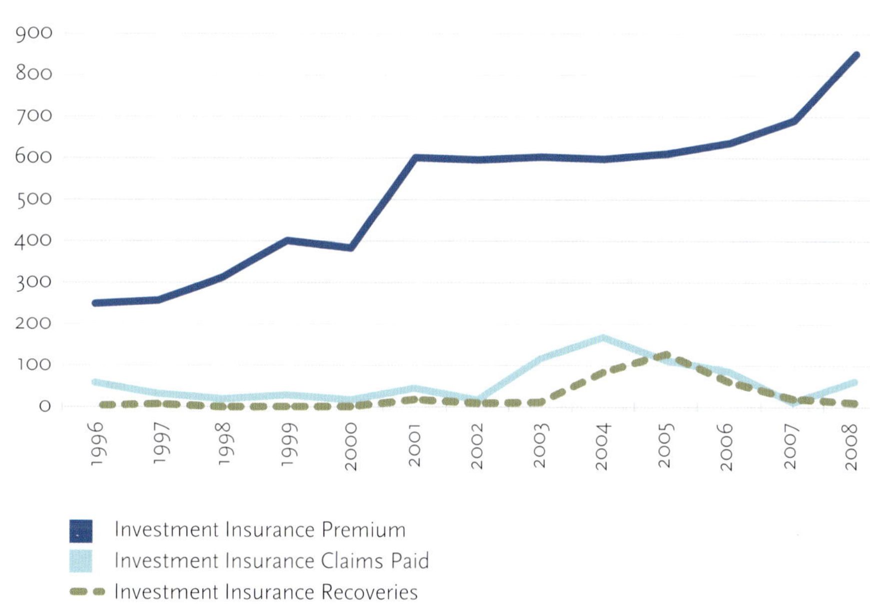

Source: Berne Union 2009.

Annex 3 MIGA-EIU Political Risk Survey 2009

The data provided below are based on a survey conducted on MIGA's behalf by the Economist Intelligence Unit (EIU). The survey was conducted in June 2009, and contains the responses of 351 executives from multinational enterprises around the world. Quota sampling was used to ensure that the industry and geographic composition of the survey sample approximate actual FDI outflows': following a first round of responses to the questionnaire, additional email campaigns targeting respondents in specific sectors or locations were conducted until all demographic quotas were met. All respondents are involved in, or familiar with, their company's investment plans in emerging markets and 47 percent describe themselves as board members or C-level executives. They represent companies with global annual revenues of $500 million or more and 37 percent exceed $10 billion on an annual basis.

What are your organisation's global annual revenues in dollars?

Percent of respondents

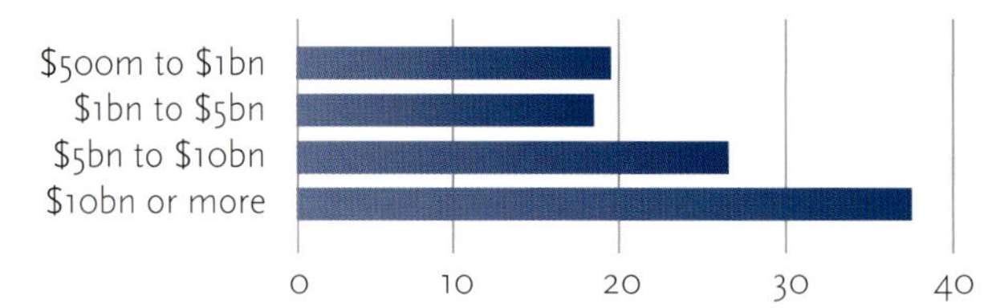

Survey Questions:

1. How do you expect your company's planned investments abroad to change this year compared with last year? And over the next three years compared with the previous three years?

Percent of respondents

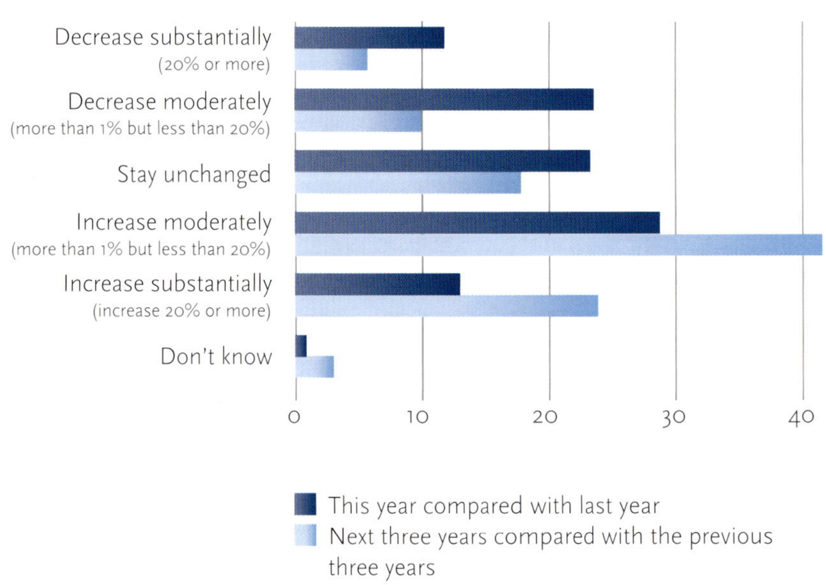

2. Do you expect your company to shift its foreign investments from emerging to developed markets, or vice versa this year? And over the next three years?

Percent of respondents

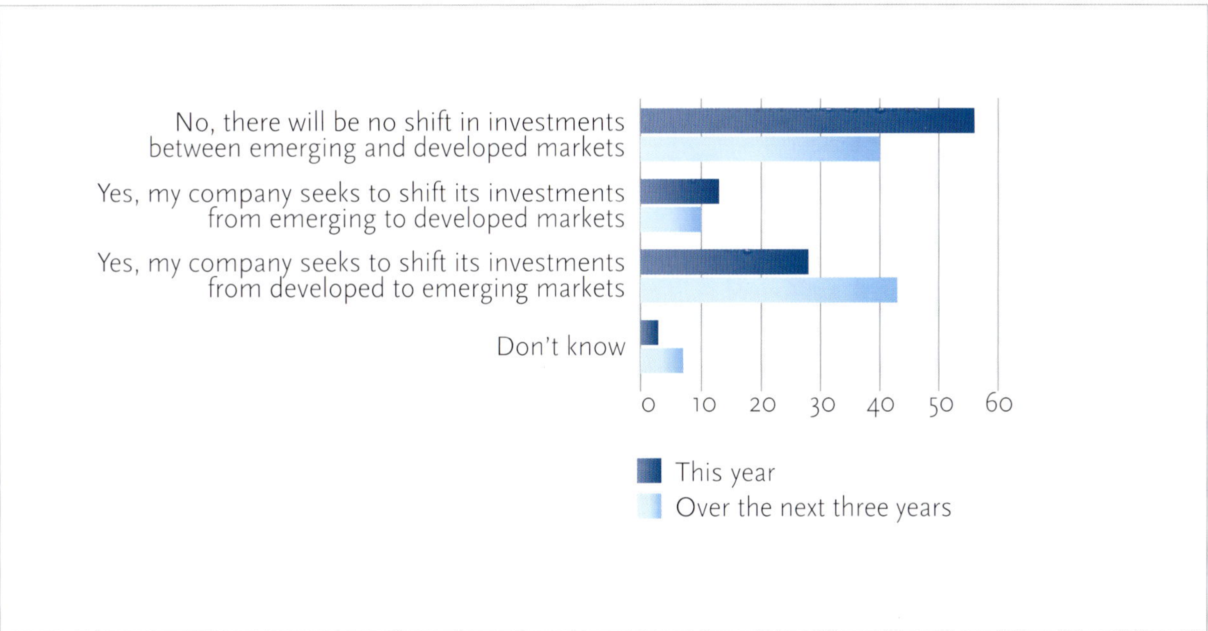

5. In your opinion, which of the following factors will pose the greatest constraint on investments by your company in emerging markets this year and over the next three years? (Select up to three)

Percent of respondents

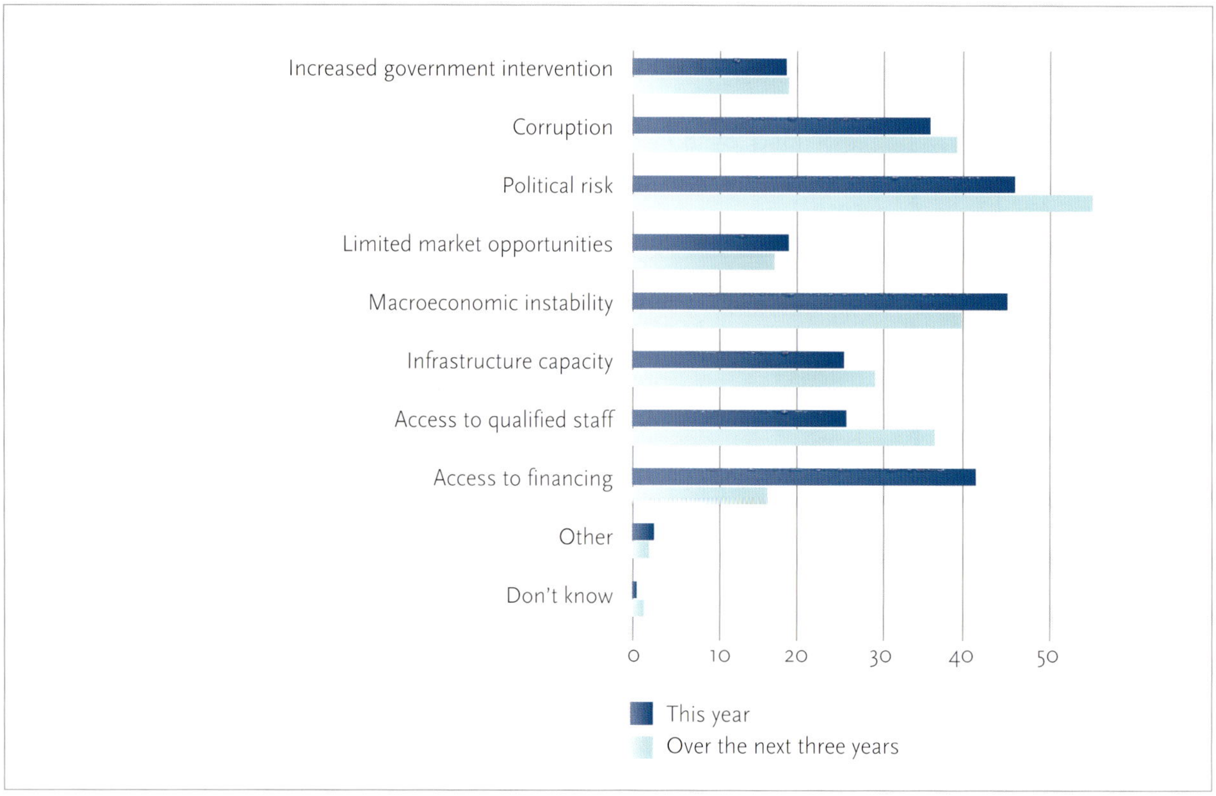

6. How has the current global financial crisis affected your company's view of the following items?

Percent of respondents

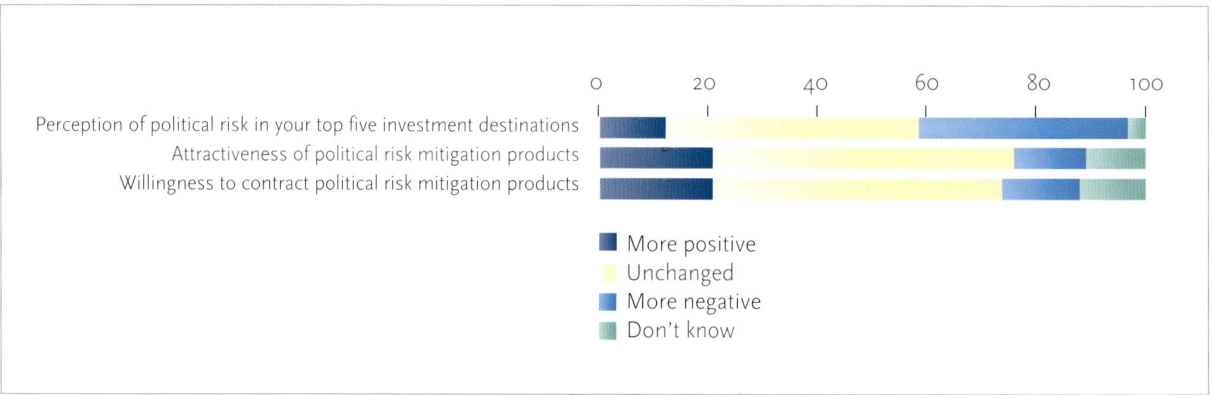

7. What is your company's overall perception of the political risks in investing in the following emerging markets?

Number of respondents, and percent

	Very high	High	Moderate	Low	Don't know	Total
Afghanistan	1 20 %	2 40 %	2 40 %	0 0 %	0 0 %	5 100 %
Algeria	3 14 %	9 41 %	8 36 %	2 9 %	0 0 %	22 100 %
Argentina	5 12 %	7 17 %	16 39 %	12 29 %	1 2 %	41 100 %
Bangladesh	1 8 %	4 33 %	5 42 %	2 17 %	0 0 %	12 100 %
Brazil	1 1 %	16 10 %	77 47 %	68 41 %	2 1 %	164 100 %
China	7 3 %	50 21 %	121 51 %	58 24 %	1 0 %	237 100 %
Colombia	1 7 %	4 27 %	5 33 %	5 33 %	0 0 %	15 100 %
Congo, Dem. Rep.	0 0 %	1 33 %	1 33 %	0 0 %	1 33 %	3 100 %
Egypt, Arab Rep.	0 0 %	7 23 %	19 61 %	5 16 %	0 0 %	31 100 %
Ethiopia	0 0 %	0 0 %	1 50 %	1 50 %	0 0 %	2 100 %
Ghana	0 0 %	2 20 %	2 20 %	6 60 %	0 0 %	10 100 %
India	2 1 %	33 16 %	94 46 %	72 35 %	3 1 %	204 100 %
Indonesia	0 0 %	6 18 %	19 58 %	8 24 %	0 0 %	33 100 %
Iran, Islamic Rep.	2 29 %	4 57 %	1 14 %	0 0 %	0 0 %	7 100 %
Iraq	3 21 %	8 57 %	2 14 %	1 7 %	0 0 %	14 100 %
Kenya	2 18 %	2 18 %	5 45 %	2 18 %	0 0 %	11 100 %
Malaysia	1 3 %	4 10 %	18 46 %	15 38 %	1 3 %	39 100 %
Mexico	1 1 %	8 11 %	32 45 %	28 39 %	2 3 %	71 100 %
Morocco	0 0 %	5 21 %	11 46 %	8 33 %	0 0 %	24 100 %
Mozambique	3 23 %	3 23 %	1 8 %	6 46 %	0 0 %	13 100 %
Nepal	0 0 %	0 0 %	0 0 %	0 0 %	0 0 %	0 100 %
Nigeria	5 28 %	7 39 %	5 28 %	1 6 %	0 0 %	18 100 %

14. In its foreign investments, does your company typically take a majority stake or does it invest in companies that are controlled by others?

Percent of respondents

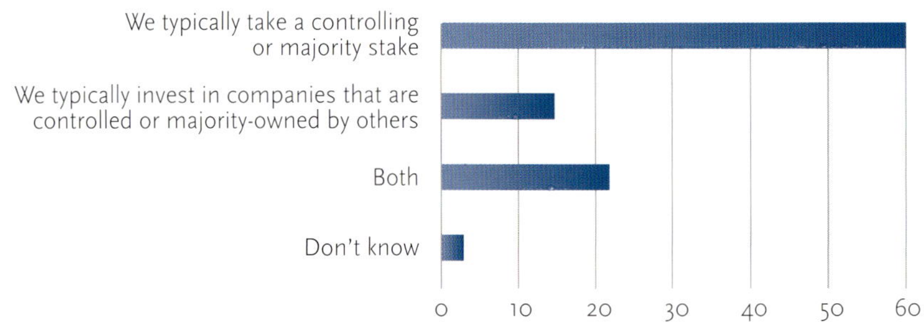

15. How would you rate your company's capabilities in the following areas?

Percent of respondents

	Excellent	Very good	Good	Weak	Non-existent	Don't know
Overall political risk assessment	11	27	45	13	2	2
Anticipating new political risks	6	22	46	22	2	2
Implementing existing political risk mitigation strategies	7	19	47	18	5	4
Evaluating new political risk mitigation strategies	5	21	39	25	4	6
Assigning roles and responsibilities for political risk management	6	21	37	23	7	6

16. How would you assess your company's average financial performance relative to its peers over the past three years?

Percent of respondents

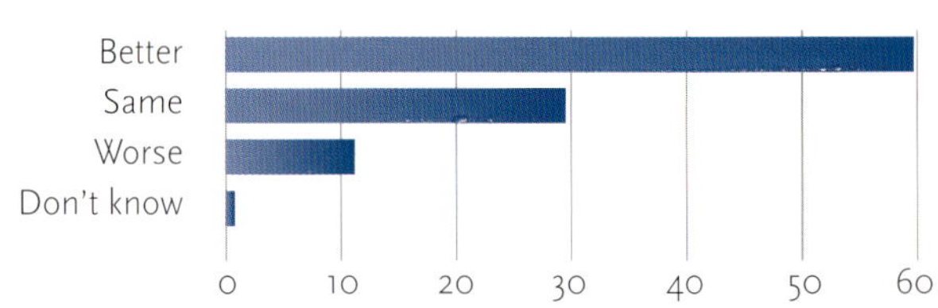

Annex 4 The MIGA-VCC Political Risk Survey in the BRICs

This survey of multinational enterprises headquartered in Brazil, the Russian Federation, India and China was carried out by the Vale Columbia Center on Sustainable International Investment (VCC) between late June and late August 2009 with the assistance of four consultants. These were Sociedade Brasileira de Estudos de Empresas Transnacionais e da Globalização Econômica (SOBEET) in Brazil; Qi Guoqiang, President, International Cooperation Journal, Ministry of Commerce, in China; Premila Nazareth, an independent consultant in India; and Andrei Panibratov at the Graduate School of Management, St. Petersburg State University in the Russian Federation.

Methodology

Initial lists of leading outward investors to be surveyed were put together by the consultants and were sent to MIGA by the VCC on June 29, 2009. The sources of the lists varied by country. In Brazil, SOBEET drew upon its own work to compile a list of 81 companies. (SOBEET carries out an annual survey of outward investors in Brazil and ranks them by a transnationalization index.) In China, a list of 85 companies was compiled in two stages. In the first, the consultant drew on the 50 largest overseas investors in the Ministry of Commerce database; in the second were added 35 participants in a conference on Chinese overseas investment strategy organized by the Chinese Academy of International Trade and Economic Cooperation (CAITEC). In India, the consultant drew upon two sources to compile a list of 42 companies. The first 24 companies on the list came from the VCC-ISB 2009 ranking of India's leading outward investors. The next 18 companies came from Grant Thornton's annual listing of Indian firms' overseas mergers and acquisitions. In the Russian Federation, 45 companies with noticeable and relatively transparent international activity were selected from the Expert RA rating agency's list of the largest Russian companies by sales.

The response rate varied by country (table 1), with Brazil having the lowest response rate (28 percent) and India the highest (55 percent). The response rate for the BRICs as a whole was 36 percent. In the case of India and the Russian Federation, the number of individuals responding was the same as the number of companies (23 and 19), while both Brazil and China had nine additional responses each, i.e., nine companies in each country returned two responses (table 1).

1. Summary of BRIC companies surveyed and responding

Number of respondents

Countries	Companies surveyed	Companies responding	Company response rate (%)	Individuals responding	Companies with more than one respondent
Brazil	81	23	28	32	9
China	85	25	32	34	9
India	42	23	55	23	0
Russian Fed.	45	19	42	19	0
Total	253	90	36	108	18

2. What are your company's global annual revenues in dollars?

Percent of respondents

Countries

	Less than $500m	Between $500m and $1bn	Between $1bn and $5bn	Between $5bn and $10bn	Over $10bn
Brazil	35	13	26	4	22
China	4	28	32	4	32
India	17	13	43	13	13
Russian Fed.	5	26	26	32	11

3. What is your company's primary industry?

Percent of respondents

Countries

	Primary	Manufacturing	Services
Brazil	9	48	43
China	16	48	36
India	4	74	22
Russian Fed.	21	37	42

4. In its foreign investments, does your company invest mostly as equity or as loans?

Percent of respondents

Countries

	Equity	Loans	Both	Don't know
Brazil	35	4	61	0
China	12	12	76	0
India	39	4	57	0
Russian Fed.	68	5	16	11

5. In its foreign investments, does your company typically take a majority stake or does it invest in companies that are controlled by others?

Percent of respondents

Countries	Choice of stake in FDI			
	Majority	Minority	Both	Don't know
Brazil	74	0	26	0
China	40	0	56	4
India	83	0	17	0
Russian Fed.	79	11	11	0

6. How would you assess your company's average financial performance relative to its peers over the past three years?

Percent of respondents

Countries	Financial performance compared to peers		
	Better	Same	Worse
Brazil	69	19	12
China	52	45	3
India	83	13	4
Russian Fed.	58	26	16

7. What are the five main emerging market destinations for your company's direct investments abroad today?

	Brazil	China	India	Russian Fed.
Top investment destinations	Argentina	Russian Fed.	China	CIS*
	Chile	Indonesia	Brazil	Kazakhstan
	Angola	Nigeria	Middle East	Ukraine
	Mexico	Pakistan	Africa	China
	Venezuela RB	Angola	Russian Fed.	Other

* *Commonwealth of Independent States.*

8. In what five Emerging Markets does your company plan the highest level of new investment over the next three years?

	Countries			
	Brazil	**China**	**India**	**Russian Fed.**
Top investment destinations	Argentina	Russian Fed.	China	China
	Mexico	Brazil	Brazil	Azerbaijan
	Angola	Indonesia	Russian Fed.	Eastern Europe
	Chile	Argentina	Middle East	n.a.
	Peru	Vietnam	South Africa	n.a.

9. How do you expect your company's planned investments abroad to change this year compared with last year?

Percent of respondents

Investment plans	Countries			
	Brazil	**China**	**India**	**Russian Fed.**
Increase substantially (20% or more)	27	17	17	5
Increase moderately (less than 20%)	23	38	30	26
Stay unchanged	31	31	43	32
Decrease moderately (less than 20%)	4	10	0	26
Decrease substantially (20% or more)	12	3	4	5
Don't know	4	0	4	5

10. How do you expect your company's planned investments abroad to change over the next three years compared with the previous three years?

Percent of respondents

Investment plans	Countries			
	Brazil	**China**	**India**	**Russian Fed.**
Increase substantially (20% or more)	36	33	35	11
Increase moderately (less than 20%)	36	42	39	26
Stay unchanged	20	12	9	37
Decrease moderately (less than 20%)	0	0	0	16
Decrease substantially (20% or more)	0	0	0	0
Don't know	8	12	17	11

11. For this year do you expect your company to shift its foreign investments from emerging to developed markets, or vice versa?

Percent of respondents

Planned shifts	Countries			
	Brazil	China	India	Russian Fed.
From emerging to developed markets	8	7	0	5
From developed to emerging markets	4	11	9	16
No shift	88	78	87	68
Don't know	0	4	4	11

12. Over the next three years do you expect your company to shift its foreign investments from emerging to developed markets, or vice versa?

Percent of respondents

Planned shifts	Countries			
	Brazil	China	India	Russian Fed.
From emerging to developed markets	4	3	5	0
From developed to emerging markets	17	10	27	5
No shift	71	69	50	58
Don't know	8	17	18	37

13. In your opinion, which five Emerging Markets are the riskiest to invest in today?

	Investor countries			
	Brazil	China	India	Russian Fed.
Investment destinations in descending order of riskiness	Venezuela RB	Iraq	Russian Fed.	CIS*
	Bolivia	Zimbabwe	Iran, Islamic Rep.	Kazakhstan
	Argentina	Sudan	Sudan	Latin America
	Russian Fed.	Korea Dem. Rep.	Africa	Middle East
	Ecuador	Indonesia	Pakistan	n.a.

* *Commonwealth of Independent States.*

14. In your opinion, which of the following factors will pose the greatest constraint on investment by your company in Emerging Markets this year? Select up to three.

Percent of respondents

Constraints	Countries			
	Brazil	China	India	Russian Fed.
Limited market opportunities	38	68	39	5
Access to financing	13	6	39	47
Access to qualified staff	19	3	22	0
Infrastructure capacity	16	44	13	47
Macroeconomic instability	53	35	43	47
Political risk	78	47	43	63
Corruption	22	35	17	11
Increased government intervention	28	12	17	0
Other	3	0	13	0
Don't know	0	0	4	79

15. In your opinion, which of the following factors will pose the greatest constraint on investment by your company in Emerging Markets over the next three years? Select up to three.

Percent of respondents

Constraints	Countries			
	Brazil	China	India	Russian Fed.
Limited market opportunities	34	44	30	5
Access to financing	13	9	30	42
Access to qualified staff	41	6	30	5
Infrastructure capacity	38	56	13	21
Macroeconomic instability	44	24	39	47
Political risk	69	68	52	42
Corruption	19	35	39	0
Increased government intervention	13	26	22	0
Other	9	0	9	0
Don't know	0	0	4	116

16. In your opinion, which types of political risk are of most concern to your company when investing in Emerging Markets this year? Select up to three.

Percent of respondents

Political risk of most concern	Countries			
	Brazil	China	India	Russian Fed.
Transfer and convertibility restrictions	56	53	61	5
Expropriation	31	29	9	42
War and civil disturbance	22	65	35	37
Terrorism	6	50	30	5
Breach of contract	59	26	39	95
Non-honoring of government guarantees	56	38	35	58
Restrictions on FDI outflows in home country	16	9	13	0
Other adverse regulatory changes	22	24	48	5

17. In your opinion, which types of political risk are of most concern to your company when investing in Emerging Markets over the next three years? Select up to three.

Percent of respondents

Political risk of most concern	Countries			
	Brazil	China	India	Russian Fed.
Transfer and convertibility restrictions	53	47	57	21
Expropriation	31	32	9	16
War and civil disturbance	28	47	35	11
Terrorism	3	59	39	0
Breach of contract	63	21	35	79
Non-honoring of government guarantees	56	32	35	37
Restrictions on FDI outflows in home country	19	6	17	5
Other adverse regulatory changes	22	24	43	11

18. How has the current global financial and economic crisis affected your company's view of the following item?

Percent of respondents

Country	Perception of risks			
	More positive	Unchanged	More negative	Don't know
Brazil	0	53	47	0
China	29	68	0	3
India	0	61	30	9
Russian Fed.	0	63	37	0

19. How has the current global financial and economic crisis affected your company's view of the following item?

Percent of respondents

Country	Attractiveness of risk mitigation products			
	More positive	Unchanged	More negative	Don't know
Brazil	22	53	13	13
China	44	47	3	6
India	13	61	4	22
Russian Fed.	21	63	5	11

20. How has the current global financial and economic crisis affected your company's view of the following item?

Percent of respondents

Country	Willingness to contract risk mitigation products			
	More positive	Unchanged	More negative	Don't know
Brazil	38	59	0	3
China	59	38	0	3
India	18	64	5	14
Russian Fed.	26	53	5	16

21. Which of the following does your company use as a tool for political risk mitigation? Select all that apply for your top five Emerging Market destinations.

Percent of respondents

Risk mitigation tool	Countries			
	Brazil	China	India	Russian Fed.
Political risk insurance	6	12	17	53
Credit default swaps	9	0	4	0
Use of third-party consultants	31	12	43	0
Engagement with host government	44	24	52	68
Engagement with local communities	25	3	39	5
Joint venture/alliance with local company	50	38	65	5
Political/economic risk analysis	47	56	43	26
Scenario planning	50	15	35	0
Engagement with NGOs	16	0	13	0
Operational hedging	3	9	17	11
Other	9	0	4	0
None	9	18	13	0
Don't know	0	3	0	5

22. For which of the following types of political risk does your company use political risk insurance in your top five Emerging Market destinations? For each country, select all that apply.

Percent of respondents

Risk covered by insurance	Countries			
	Brazil	China	India	Russian Fed.
Transfer and convertibility restrictions	9	12	17	0
Expropriation	6	12	9	5
War and civil disturbance	3	6	0	11
Terrorism	3	6	0	0
Breach of contract	9	6	4	53
Non-honoring of government guarantees	6	0	13	5
Restrictions on FDI outflows in home country	3	0	4	0
Other adverse regulatory changes	3	0	9	11

23. What are the primary reasons your company does not use tools or products to mitigate political risks? Select all that apply.

Percent of respondents

Reason for not mitigating political risk	Countries			
	Brazil	China	India	Russian Fed.
Low level of political risk	41	38	48	16
Lack of appropriate tools and products	50	59	39	42
Cost of tools and products	31	12	13	11
Cumbersome contracting process	22	6	9	11
Unaware of tools and products	31	29	35	11
Other	6	0	4	0
Don't know	3	0	9	16

24. Moving forward, do you expect your company to consider political risk insurance for its investments abroad?

Percent of respondents

Countries			
	Yes	No	Don't know
Brazil	35	27	38
China	79	14	7
India	65	4	30
Russian Fed.	32	37	32

Annex 5 FDI and Political Risk: A Review of the Academic Literature

Research findings are mixed when looking at the link between political risk and FDI. Early studies on the association between FDI and political risk (e.g. Kobrin 1979) found the effects of political instability on different measures of FDI to be inconsistent. Subsequent econometric studies continued to produce mixed findings. A stream of studies showed that political risk is negatively correlated with the flow of FDI (Schneider and Frey 1985, Lim 2001, Nonnenberg and Cardoso 2004, Busse and Hefeker 2005). In these studies, political risk typically featured as one of several determinants of the location of FDI. Nigh (1985), analyzing 24 countries over 21 years, found that both inter-nation and intra-nation conflict and cooperation negatively affected manufacturing FDI flows by U.S. firms. In a cross-sectional analysis of FDI flows to 36 countries for 1977 and 1982, Loree and Guisinger (1995) found that political stability significantly promoted FDI inflows in 1982, but not in 1977. Using data from all reported manufacturing plant openings from 1984 to 1987, Woodward and Rolfe (1993) found that political stability increases the probability of a country being selected as an investment location. Li (2005) looked at how different forms of political violence affect FDI for a large group of countries, and found that the impact on FDI is very much determined by whether political violence is anticipated or not, with unanticipated events having a strong negative effect on FDI. Finally Meon and Sekkat (2008) raised the issue that the sensitivity of foreign investors to political risk in a particular country depends on the amount of capital available for investment at a given point in time; when FDI is booming, investors are less sensitive to political risk.

Another set of studies have found political risk not to be a significant determinant of FDI. For example, Fatehi-Sedeh and Safizadeh (1989) did not find a statistical association between political stability and FDI. Olibe and Crumbley (1997) did not find consistent evidence that an index of political risk influences U.S. FDI flows to 10 out of 13 OPEC countries. Li and Resnick (2003) found that political instability does not have a statistically significant effect on FDI, yet "regime durability" encourages such investment. Wheeler and Mody (1992) reported that political risk had little importance in United States MNE location decisions. Similar results were reported by Asiedu (2002) and Bevan and Estrin (2000) on different subgroups of countries. More recently, in a pooled analysis of 52 developing countries between 1982 and 1995, Sethi, Guisinger, Phelan and Berg (2003) found that political instability, measured by a composite variable on a 100-point scale, did not influence U.S. FDI flows to 28 countries between 1981 and 2000. Globerman and Shapiro (2003) found that an index of political instability and violence, including armed conflict, social unrest, terrorist threats etc., did not influence the probability of a country receiving any FDI, but reduced the amount of FDI a country actually received. Bevan and Estrin (2004) found political risk in a host country not to be a significant determinant of FDI for transition economies.

While a degree of ambiguity exists when it comes to the relationship between political risk variables and FDI based on econometric studies, findings based on surveys unequivocally support the view that MNEs do take into account political risk in their investment decisions. Early studies (e.g., Aharoni, 1966, Bass, McGreggor and Walters, 1977) showed that both political risk and political stability featured prominently in investment decisions. Porcano (1993) found that the political climate of a host country consistently ranked above 3 on a 5-point importance scale in a survey of Canadian, United Kingdom and Japanese firms across 36 industries.

In recent years there has been growing evidence that political risk not only features in investment decisions, but is also moving towards the top of corporate agendas, as reflected in various business surveys. An Economist Intelligence Unit survey of 602 investors conducted in 2007 found that companies expected political risk to become a much greater problem for investments in the future than in the recent past, especially in emerging markets (World Investment Prospects to 2011, 2007). A survey by Ernst & Young identified political risk as the main investment constraint for companies based in developed countries (Ernst & Young, 2007). A report from Lloyd's, in cooperation with the Economist Intelligence Unit, found that global businesses were becoming more concerned about risks from political violence. More than one third of 154 survey takers said that they were avoiding overseas investments for fear of political violence (Lloyd's (2007)). A report by Grant Thornton (2008) based on survey evidence found political and economic stability to be of equal importance with market size and growth potential when determining the location of FDI. A survey by Atradius and EIU (2008) found that political instability tops the list of government or bureaucratic obstacles in emerging markets. Finally, the Economist Intelligence Unit's Business Environment Rankings (BER) model, which seeks to measure the attractiveness of a country's business environment based on the relative weight of multiple criteria used by companies in their investment decision, found that only policy directed explicitly at FDI and the total BER score (which captures the fact that many of the BER components have a complementary effect) appear to have a more powerful influence on FDI than political risk, compared with all other determinants.

Annex 6 PRI Providers

Berne Union members

Public		
Company	Economy	Year joined
ASEI	Indonesia	1999
ASHRA	Israel	1958
CESCE	Spain	1972
ECGC	India	1957
ECGD	United Kingdom	1934
ECIC SA	South Africa	2004
EFIC	Australia	1957
EGAP	Czech Republic	1996
EKF	Denmark	1997
EKN	Sweden	1947
EXIMBANKA SR	Slovak Republic	2004
EXIM J	Jamaica	1983
FINNVERA	Finland	1964
GIEK	Norway	1951
HKEC	Hong Kong SAR, China	1969
KEIC	Korea, Rep. of	1977
KUKE	Poland	1997
MEHIB	Hungary	1998
MEXIM	Malaysia	1985
NEXI	Japan	1970
ONDD	Belgium	1954
OPIC	United States	1974
SACE	Italy	1959
SERV	Switzerland	1956
SID	Slovenia	1998
SINOSURE	China	1996
SLECIC	Sri Lanka	1984
TEBC	Taiwan, China	1996
THAI EXIMBANK	Thailand	2003
TURK EXIMBANK	Turkey	1992
US EXIMBANK	United States	1962

Multilateral		
Company	Economy	Year joined
ICIEC	Multilateral	2007
MIGA	Multilateral	1992

Private		
Company	Economy	Year joined
ATRADIUS	Netherlands	1953
CGIC	South Africa	1958
CHARTIS	United States	1999
CHUBB	United States	2004
COFACE	France	1948
COSEC	Portugal	1977
CREDSURE	Zimbabwe	1983
ECICS	Singapore	1979
EH GERMANY	Germany	1953
FCIA	United States	1963
HISCOX	United Kingdom	2008
OEKB	Austria	1955
PWC	Germany	1974
SBCE	Brazil	2001
SOVEREIGN	Bermuda	2001
ZURICH	United States	2001

Lloyds Syndicate members

ACE Global Markets	Hiscox
Amlin	Kiln
Ark	Liberty Syn Mgmt
Ascot	Limit
Beazley	MAP
C.V. Starr	Marketform
Catlin	Novae
Chaucer	Talbot
Hardy	QBE

Annex 6 PRI Providers (cont'd)

Prague Club members*

Public		
Company	Country	Year joined
AOFI	Serbia	2007
BAEZ	Bulgaria	1997
BECI	Botswana	2005
ECGA	Oman	2000
ECGE	Egypt, Arab Rep.	2003
ECIC SA	South Africa	2002
ECIE	United Arab Emirates	2009
EGAP	Czech Rep.	1993
EGFI	Iran, Islamic Rep.	1999
EXIM R	Romania	1993
EXIMBANKA SR	Slovak Rep.	1993
EXIMGARANT	Belarus	1999
HBOR	Croatia	1997
IGA	Bosnia and Herzegovina	1999
JLGC	Jordan	2001
KECIC	Kazakhstan	2004
KREDEX	Estonia	1999
KUKE	Poland	1993
MBDP	Macedonia, FYR	1999
MEHIB	Hungary	1993
NAIFE	Sudan	2007
PHILEXIM	Philippines	1997
SEP	Saudi Arabia	2000
SID	Slovenia	1993
THAI EXIMBANK	Thailand	1997
UKREXIMBANK	Ukraine	2008
UZBEKINVEST	Uzbekistan	1996
VNESHECO NOMBANK	Russian Fed.	2008

Private		
Company	Country	Year joined
LCI	Lebanon	2009
Multilateral		
Company	Country	Year joined
ATI	Multilateral	2002
DHAMAN	Multilateral	2000
ICIEC	Multilateral	2001

* *Not all members are providers of investment PRI.*

Annex 7 Selected Factors Affecting Pricing in the PRI Industry

Country Risk: Insurers usually define a base price for host countries based on risk, reflecting macroeconomic, social, political, institutional, governance and geopolitical factors.

Insurance and reinsurance capacity: The aggregate exposure to a country influences the pricing of new policies, especially when country capacity limits are being reached. High PRI demand usually translates into increased prices; the industry's capacity for a country is inversely related to perceptions of country risk.

Industry/Sector: Within a country, the price of PRI can vary significantly across industries based on risk perceptions. Projects that depend on government actions or guarantees tend to be perceived as higher risk as in the case of projects involving natural resources.

Claims/Loss Experience: Elevated claims levels result in higher prices, especially in the short term.

Profile of the Insured: The likelihood of claims can be influenced by the actions of the insured, such as its stance on security, its ability to deal with host governments, its conformity with laws and its engagement with local communities. The nationality of the investor can also affect the likelihood of problems materializing.

Project Development Benefits: Projects with positive developmental impacts are considered less risky than others; environmental and social issues can lead to negative reactions in host countries.

Coverage Required: The types of perils and the number of risks covered influences the price.

Tenor of the Policy: Prices increase with the length of the insurance commitment.

Portfolio Commitments: Insurers are always wary of the potential for adverse selection (where coverage is sought only for the riskiest countries) in PRI. Therefore, they may be willing to offer more competitive prices when insuring a whole diversified corporate portfolio of investments in different countries.

BIBLIOGRAPHY

Aharoni, Yair. 1966. *The Foreign Investment Decision Process*. Boston, MA: Harvard University.

Alwis, Athula, Vladimir Kremerman, Yakov Lantsman, Jason Harger and Junning Shi. 2007. "Political Risk Reinsurance Pricing – A Capital Market Approach." Paper presented at the 28th International Congress of Actuaries, Paris, May 29-June 2.

Asiedu, Elizabeth. 2002. "On the Determinants of Foreign Direct Investment to Developing Countries: Is Africa Different?" *World Development* 30: 107-119.

Atradius and EIU. 2008. *Promise or Peril? The Lure of the Emerging Markets*. London: Economist Intelligence Unit.

Bailey, David. 2004. "Commentary on Finding Common Ground or Uncommon Solutions: A Private Provider's View." In *International Political Risk Management: The Brave New World*, ed. Theodore H. Moran, 177-180. Washington, DC: World Bank.

Bass, Bernard M., Donald W. McGregor and James L. Walters. 1977. "Selecting Foreign Plant Sites: Economic, Social and Political Considerations." *Academy of Management Journal* 20: 535-551.

Beers, David and Marie Cavanaugh. 2008. "Sovereign Credit Ratings: A Primer." Research Paper, Standard & Poor's, New York.

Berry, Charles. 2006. "Interview With Charles Berry." *Political Risk Insurance Newsletter* II (I): 1-3.

Berry, Charles. 2008. "The Convergence of the Terrorism Insurance and Political Risk Insurance Markets for Emerging Market Risk: Why it is Necessary and How it Will Come About." In *International Political Risk Management: Needs of the Present, Challenges of the Future*, ed. Theodore H. Moran, Gerald T. West and Keith Martin, 13-35. Washington, DC: World Bank.

Bevan, Alan A. and Saul Estrin. 2004. "The Determinants of Foreign Direct Investment into European Transition Economies." *Journal of Comparative Economics* 32 (4): 775-787.

Bremmer, Ian and Robert Johnston. 2009. "The Rise and Fall of Resource Nationalism." *Survival: Global Politics and Strategy* 51 (2): 149–158.

Brown, Vivian. 2004. "Political Risk Insurance after September 11 and the Argentine Crisis: A Public Provider's Perspective." In *International Political Risk Management: The Brave New World*, ed. Theodore H. Moran, 15-25. Washington, DC: World Bank.

Busse, Matthias and Carsten Hefeker. 2005. "Political Risk, Institutions and Foreign Direct Investment." April, HWWA Discussion Paper 315, University of Bochum. http://papers.ssrn.com/sol3/papers.cfm?abstract_id=704283

Cavanaugh, Marie, Benjamin Young and YeeFarn Phua. 2009. *Sovereign Ratings And Country T&C Assessments*. New York: Standard & Poor's.

Cheng, Leonard K. and Zihui Ma. Forthcoming. "China's Outward FDI: Past and Future." In *China's Growing Role in World Trade*, ed. Robert Feenstra and Shang-Jin Way. Chicago: The University of Chicago Press.

Control Risks. 2007. *The Terrorist Threat and the War On Terror Five Years On*. London: Control Risks.

Davies, Kenneth. 2009. "While Global FDI Falls, China's Outward FDI Doubles." *Columbia FDI Perspectives* 5 (May).

Deloitte. 2008. *Russian Multinationals: New Players in the Global Economy*. Moscow: Deloitte.

EIU and the Columbia Program on International Investment. 2006. *World Investment Prospects to 2010: Boom or Backlash?* London: Economist Intelligence Unit.

EIU and the Columbia Program on International Investment. 2007. *World Investment Prospects to 2011: Foreign Direct Investment and the Challenge of Political Risk*. London: Economist Intelligence Unit.

Ernst & Young. 2007. *Risk Management in Emerging Markets*. London: Ernst & Young.

Eurasia Group. 2009. "Eurasia Group Global Trends Quarterly, Second Quarter 2009." London: PriceWaterhouseCoopers.

Fatehi-Siedeh, K. and Hossein M. Safizadeh. 1989. "The Association Between Political Instability and Flow of Foreign Direct Investment." *Management International Review* 27: 4-13.

Fundação Dom Cabral and Vale Columbia Center on Sustainable International Investment. 2007. "Brazil's Multinationals Take Off." Press Release, December 3.

Globerman, Steven and Daniel Shapiro. 2003. "Governance Infrastructure and US Foreign Direct Investment." *Journal of International Business Studies* 34: 19-40.

Grant Thornton. 2008. *Emerging Markets: Reshaping the Global Economy. International Business Report 2008.* Chicago: Grant Thorton.

Gurría, Angel. 2009. "The Crisis and its Impact on Cross Border Investment." Remarks by Angel Gurría, OECD Secretary-General, during a lunch organized by the United States Council for International Business, Washington, DC, June 2.

Handami, Kausar, Elise Liebers and George Zanjani. 2005. "An Overview of Political Risk Insurance." New York: Federal Reserve Bank of New York.

Hansen, Kenneth W. 2004. "Investment Promotion and Political Risk Insurance." Paper presented at conference, "Encouraging Capital Flows Into Africa," Johannesburg, South Africa, September 29-30.

Hansen, Kenneth W. 2005. "Tales from the Dark Side: Lessons Learned from Troubled Investments." In *International Political Risk Management: Looking to the Future*, ed. Theodore H. Moran and Gerald T. West, 12-29. Washington, DC: World Bank.

Heppel, Toby. 2005. "Perspectives on Private-Public Relationships in Political Risk Insurance." In *International Political Risk Management: Looking to the Future*, ed. Theodore H. Moran and Gerald T. West, 139-157. Washington, DC: World Bank.

IMF. 2009. "IMF Lending Arrangements as of September 30, 2009."
http://www.imf.org/external/np/fin/tad/extarr11.aspx?memberKey1=ZZZZ&date1key=2020-02-28

Indian School of Business and Vale Columbia Center on Sustainable International Investment. 2009. "The Growth Story of Indian Multinationals."
http://www.vcc.columbia.edu/documents/IndianMNEReport-Final.pdf

Jensen, Nathan M. 2006. "Political Regimes and Political Risk: Democratic Institutions and Expropriation Risk for Multinational Investors." November, Working Paper, Washington University.
http://ssrn.com/abstract=869460

Jordan, Michael. 2004. "Assessment of the Availability of Political Risk Insurance for Infrastructure Investments." May, unpublished report for the Private Infrastructure Development Group.

Kekic, Laza. 2009. "The Global Economic Crisis and FDI Flows to Emerging Markets." *Columbia FDI Perspectives* 15 (October).

Kobrin, Stephen J. 1979. "Political Risk: A Review and Reconsideration." *Journal of International Business Studies* 10: 67 - 80.

KPMG. 2009. "Emerging Markets Continue to Narrow the M&A Gap." KPMG.
http://www.kpmg.com/Global/IssuesAndInsights/ArticlesAndPublications/Pages/Emerging-markets-continue-to-narrow-the-MA-gap.aspx

Li, Quan and Adam Resnick. 2003. "Reversal of Fortunes: Democracy, Property Rights and Foreign Direct Investment Inflows in Developing Countries." *International Organization* 57 (1): 175-214.

Li, Quan. 2005. "Political Violence and Foreign Direct Investment." *Regional Economic Integration* 12: 225-249.

Lim, Ewe-Ghee. 2001. "Determinants of, and the Relation Between, Foreign Direct Investment and Growth: A Summary of the Recent Literature." IMF Working Paper 01/175.
http://ssrn.com/abstract=880230

Lima, Louis A. and Octavio de Barros. 2009. "The Growth of Brazil's Direct Investment Abroad and the Challenges it Faces." *Columbia FDI Perspectives* 13 (August).

Lloyd's. 2007. Lloyds 360. *Under Attack? Global Business and the Threat of Political Violence.* London: Lloyd's.

Lloyd's and Control Risks. 2009. *Lloyds 360 Insurance Market. Global Recession: The Magnifying Glass for Political Instability.* London: Lloyd's.

Loree, David W. and Stephen E. Guisinger. 1995. "Policy and Non-Policy Determinants of U.S. Equity Foreign Direct Investment." *Journal of Business Studies* 26: 281-299.

Luo, Yadong, 2008. "Political Risk and Country Risk in International Business: Concepts and Measures." In *Oxford Handbook of International Business* (2nd edition), ed. Rugman, A. M. 740-764. Oxford: Oxford University Press.

Luo, Yadong, Qiuzhi Xue and Binjie Han. Forthcoming. "How Emerging Market Governments Promote Outward FDI: Experience from China." *Journal of World Business.*

Meon, Pierre-Guillaume and Khalid Sekkat. 2008. "FDI Waves, Waves of Neglect of Political Risk." Paper presented at the "25th Symposium on Money, Banking and Finance," Luxembourg, June 18-20.

Meron, Theodor. 1976. *Investment Insurance in International Law.* New York: Oceana Publications.

Minor, Michael S. 1994. "The Demise of Expropriation as an Instrument of LDC Policy, 1980-1992." *Journal of International Business Studies* 25: 177–188.

Moran, Theodore H. 2004. "Political Risk Insurance Providers: In the Aftermath of the September 11 and Argentine Crisis." In *International Political Risk Management: The Brave New World*, ed. Theodore H. Moran, 7-14. Washington, DC: World Bank.

Moscow School of Management Skolkovo and Vale Columbia Center on Sustainable International Investment. 2008. "Emerging Russian Multinationals: Achievements and Challenges." *Moscow School of Management Skolkovo* (November).

Nigh, Douglas. 1985. "The Effect of Political Events on United States Direct Foreign Investment: A Pooled Time-Series Cross-Sectional Analysis." *Journal of International Business Studies* 16: 1-17.

Nonnenberg, Marcelo José Braga and Mario Jorge Cardoso Mendonca. 2004. "The Determinants of Direct Foreign Investment in Developing Countries." January, Working Paper, Institute of Applied Economic Research. http://ssrn.com/abstract=525462

OECD. 2009. "Global Downturn Causes Slump in Cross-Border Investment, Says OECD." Press Release, June 24.

OECD, UNCTAD and WTO. 2009. *Report on G-20 Trade and Investment Measures.* New York and Geneva: United Nations.

Oliba, K.O. and C.L. Crumbley. 1997. "Determinants of U.S. Private Foreign Direct Investments in OPEC Nations: From Public and Non-Public Policy Perspectives." *Journal of Public Budgeting, Accounting and Financial Management* 9: 331-355.

Porcano, Thomas M. 1993. "Factors Affecting the Foreign Direct Investment Decision of Firms From and Into Major Industrialized Countries." *Multinational Business Review* 1: 26-36.

Pradhan, Jaya Prakash. 2009. "Indian FDI Falls in Global Economic Crisis: Indian Multinationals Tread Cautiously." *Columbia FDI Perspectives* 11 (August).

PriceWaterhouseCoopers. 2007. "Political Risk Insurance Study." Unpublished report prepared for MIGA.

Ratha, Dilip, Sanket Mohapatra and Ani Silwal. 2009. "Migration and Remittance Trends 2009: A Better-than-Expected Outcome so Far, but Significant Risks Ahead." *Migration and Development Brief* 11 (November).
Reserve Bank of India. 2009. "Indian Investment Abroad in Joint Ventures and Wholly Owned Subsidiaries: 2009-10." Reserve Bank of India (October).

Sachs, Jeffrey D. 2007. "Addressing Political Risk in the Energy Sector." In *World Investment Prospects to 2011: Foreign Direct Investment and the Challenge of Political Risk.* EIU and the Columbia Program on International Investment, 80-83. London: Economist Intelligence Unit.

Salinger, John J. 2004. "The Impact of September 11 on Trade Credit and Political Risk Insurance: A Private Insurer's Perspective from New York." *In International Political Risk Management: The Brave New World*, ed. Theodore H. Moran, 39-44. Washington, DC: World Bank.

Sauvant, Karl P. 2009. "FDI Protectionism is on the Rise." Policy Research Working Paper 5052, World Bank, Washington, DC.

Schneider, Friedrich and Bruno S. Frey. 1985. "Economic and Political Determinants of Foreign Direct Investment." *World Development* 13 (2): 161-175.

Sethi, D., S.E. Guisinger, S.E. Phelan and D.M. Berg. 2003. "Trends in Foreign Direct Investment Flows: A Theoretical and Empirical Analysis." *Journal of International Business Studies*, 34: 315-326.

Simonian, Haig. 2009. "The Reinsurer With a Plan to Reassure." *Financial Times*, July 20.

Sinosure. 2007. "The Business of Investment Insurance in China." World Bank. http://www.pri-center.com/documents/south_south/china07.pdf

Skolkovo Institute for Emerging Market Studies. 2009. "Global Expansion of Emerging Multinationals: Post-Crisis Adjustment." *Moscow School of Management Skolkovo* (May).

Standard and Poor's. 2009. "Emerging Market Sovereign Credit: The House Shook But It's Still Standing." *S&P Credit Research* (September).

Suma, Athreye and Sandeep Kapur. 2009. "The Internationalization of Chinese and Indian Firms—Trends, Motivations and Strategy." *Industrial and Corporate Change* 18 (2): 209-221.

Thomson, Stephen. 2009. "Keeping Markets Open at Times of Economic Crisis." *OECD Policy Brief* (April).

UNCTAD. 2004. *World Investment Report 2004: The Shift Towards Services*. New York and Geneva: United Nations.

UNCTAD. 2006. *World Investment Report 2006. FDI from Developing and Transition Economies: Implications for Development*. New York and Geneva: United Nations.

UNCTAD. 2009a. "Historical Perspective, Recent Trends and Elements of Protection in International Investment Agreements." Unpublished report prepared for MIGA.

UNCTAD. 2009b. *Investment Policy Developments in G-20 Countries*. New York and Geneva: United Nations.

UNCTAD. 2009c. *World Investment Prospects Survey 2009-2011*. New York and Geneva: United Nations.

UNCTAD. 2009d. *World Investment Report 2009: Transnational Corporations, Agricultural Production and Development*. New York and Geneva: United Nations.

Vernon, Raymond. 1971. *Sovereignty at Bay: The Multinational Spread of US Enterprises*. New York: Basic Books.

Weigand, Matthew. 2009. "How to Attract International Investment in a Global Recession." *Korea IT Times*, February 13. http://www.koreaittimes.com/story/how-attract-international-investment-global-recession

Wells, Louis T, Jr. 2005. "The New International Property Rights: Can the Foreign Investor Rely on Them?" In *International Political Risk Management: Looking to the Future*, ed. Theodore H. Moran and Gerald T. West, 87-102. Washington, DC: World Bank.

Wheeler, David and Ashoka Mody. 1992. "International Investment Location Decisions: The Case of US Firms." *Journal of International Economics* 33 (1-2): 57-76.

Wiener, Jarrod. 1996. "The Transnational Political Economy: A Framework for Analysis." Lex Mercatoria. http://www.jus.uio.no/lm/the.transnational.political.economy.a.framework.for.analysis.jarrod.wiener.ukc/portrait.pdf

Woodward, Douglas P. and Robert J Rolfe. 1993. "The Location of Export-Oriented Foreign Direct Investment in the Caribbean Basin." *Journal of International Business Studies* 24 (1): 121-144.

World Bank. 2006. *Global Development Finance: The Development Potential of Surging Capital Flows*. Washington, DC: World Bank.

World Bank. 2009. Global Development Finance: *Charting a Global Recovery*. Washington, DC: World Bank.